The
Seduction Novel
of the
Early Nation

The Seduction Novel
of the Early Nation

A Call for
Socio-Political Reform

Donna R. Bontatibus

Michigan State University Press
East Lansing

∞ The paper used in this publication meets the minimum
requirements of ANSI/NISO Z39.48–1992 (R 1997) (Permanence
of Paper).

Michigan State University Press
East Lansing, Michigan 48823-5202

04 03 02 01 00 99 1 2 3 4 5 6 7 8 9

Printed and bound in the United States of America

LIBRARY OF CONGRESS CATALOGING-IN-PUBLICATION DATA

Bontatibus, Donna R., 1968-
    The seduction novel of the early nation : a call for socio-political
reform / Donna R. Bontatibus.
        p. cm.
    ISBN 0-87013-509-0 (alk. paper)
    1. American fiction—Women authors—History and criticism. 2. Seduction
in literature. 3. Feminism and literature—United States—History—19th cen-
tury. 4. Feminism and literature—United States—History—18th century. 5.
Murray, Judith Sargent, 1751-1820—Criticism and interpretation. 6. Foster,
Hannah Webster, 1759-1840—Criticism and interpretation. 7. Tenney,
Tabitha, 1762-1837—Criticism and interpretation. 8. Rowson, Mrs., 1762-
1824—Criticism and interpretation. 9. Women and literature—United
States—History—18th century. 10. Women and literature—United States—
History—19th century. I. Title.
PS374.S42 B66 1999
    813'.2093538—dc21   99-6796
                                                                          CIP

Book and cover design by Nicolette Rose

Cover illustration: *The Three Sisters*, 1783, by Benjamin West. Courtesy of the
Nelson-Atkins Museum of Art, Kansas City, Missouri.

Visit Michigan State University Press on the World Wide Web at:
www.msu.edu/unit/msupress

Contents

Introduction
Early American Seduction Novels

THROUGHOUT LITERARY HISTORY, the motifs of rape, incest, and seduction have provided the staple of Biblical stories, Greek myth and tragedy, Scottish ballads, English novels, and even contemporary romances. The titillating theme of seduction, although at times the center of scandal and controversy, also provided the staple of the first early American novels. In particular, the notable late eighteenth-century New England novelists Susanna Rowson (1762–1824), Hannah Webster Foster (1758–1840), Judith Sargent Murray (1751–1820), and Tabitha Tenney (1762–1837) all capitalized upon this fascinating theme by intertwining it with sentimental plots about young, single, middle- and upper-class women.

For years the most popular novels of the early nation—*The Power of Sympathy* (Brown 1789), *Charlotte Temple* (Rowson 1794), and *The Coquette* (Foster 1797)—were regarded as formulaic novels of victimization that mapped out a journey of seduction, abandonment, and death that women travel when they become the passive prey of scheming rakes. Certainly, many of the seducers met in the novels of Rowson, Foster, Murray, and Tenney are based upon the prototype of Samuel Richardson's Lovelace and contain other stock characters and scenes typical of the seduction narrative; however, simply to dismiss the seduction narratives by these four writers as formulaic fiction would be to dismiss the complex historical, cultural, political, and psychological issues, concerns, and debates that characterized the emergence of a new nation and its literature.

Indeed, sentimental novels with a seduction plot had a place in the new republic. In *Sensational Designs* Jane Tompkins argues that early American literature should be explored because it offers "powerful

examples of the way a culture thinks about itself, articulating and proposing solutions for the problems that shape a particular historical
moment" (1985, xi). Similarly, Cathy Davidson notes in *Revolution
and The Word* the importance of the novel to Americans "as a political
and cultural forum, a means to express their own vision of a developing
nation" and so join the debates over legal and educational reform (1986,
10–11). The literature of the early nation certainly reflected various
aspects of culture as well as the political concerns of a new nation. But
what does the sentimental novel with a seduction plot in particular
reveal about how early American culture viewed itself? What problems
were these novels addressing and what were some of their proposed solutions? More importantly, for whom were sentimental novels written and
whose problems were they addressing? At a fundamental level, we might
ask: What were the conditions that encouraged the reproduction of the
seduction plot in novel after novel and story after story?

Many eighteenth-century American novelists were influenced by the
themes popularized by Lawrence Sterne, Samuel Richardson, Henry
Fielding, and other European writers. In particular, Richardson's
Clarissa (Richardson [1747/8] 1962) captivated many American readers
and writers. When Rowson, Murray, Foster, and Tenney adopted victims
and victimizers as staples of their own fiction, they expressed their overt
familiarity with *Clarissa*.[1] In fact, by allowing characters to critique
Richardson's story, Murray and Foster included direct commentary
about Clarissa and Lovelace within their own novels. Lovelace and
Clarissa were so well known to American novel readers and writers
that even John Adams expressed his apt and intriguing familiarity
with the works of Richardson when he went as far as likening America
to Clarissa and democracy to Lovelace. Rather suspicious of democracy

---

1.   In *The Sentimental Novel in America 1789–1860*, Herbert Ross Brown
offers a discussion of the intense demand for both English and American novels
in circulating libraries and on subscription lists during the late eighteenth century. Part of this demand was for novels written by Richardson, the demand for
which was so great that Brown concludes, "Richardson was a household name
wherever novels were discussed" (1940, 29). Brown offers a sampling of reader-
responses to Richardson's novels and provides insights upon how *Clarissa* and
Pamela were often used as conduct literature—literature defining proper and
improper behavior for the privileged.

at that point in history, Adams feared that if America embraced democracy, "the rake who thinks himself handsome and well-made, and who has little faith in virtue," she would be misled by unrestrained passion and power and would ultimately embrace the same fate as did Clarissa (Fliegelman 1982, 237). Adams failed to understand that America, at that point, was already a fallen woman, not because she was seduced and abandoned by the hope of democracy, but because she expressed filial disobedience in a war for independence.

Indeed, American readers were so intrigued by fallen women that this fashionable theme permeated the periodical literature of the late eighteenth and the early nineteenth centuries, the period in which the seduction genre attained the most popularity with the middle class. The avid readers of the early nation could be captivated by a seduction story in the *Massachusetts Magazine* titled "Amelia or the Faithless Briton" (October 1789) or intrigued by such tales and essays in the *Columbian Magazine* as "The Flirt: A Moral Tale" (June 1791), "A Vindication of the Fair Sex Against the Charge of Preferring Coxcombs to Men of Worth" (July 1792), or "An Admonition to Those Who Glory in Seducing the Affection of the Fair, and Then Deserting Them" (November 1792). Many female readers of the *Lady's Weekly Miscellany* were inundated with warnings and counsel about rakes and debauchery in "A Young Lady to Her Seducer" (April 1807), "On Seduction" (October 1807), "Thoughts on Seduction" (November 1806), and "The Victim of Seduction" (November 1806). Perhaps all these tales, essays, and stories on seduction published in periodical literature inspired one pseudonymous contributor to the *New York Magazine* to formulate "The Philosophy of Coquetry" (November 1796). Although the periodical literature of the northeastern United States during the late eighteenth and early nineteenth centuries resonated with fantastic tales of seduction, the seduction plot achieved its fullest development in the sentimental novel and perhaps its most memorable development in America's first and second best-selling novels— *Charlotte Temple* and *The Coquette*.[2]

---

2. A number of scholars, including Cathy Davidson in *Revolution and The Word*, attest to the fact that *Charlotte Temple* was the first best-selling American novel in the early nation. This statistic is based upon the number of editions

The formation of novels such as *Charlotte Temple* and *The Coquette* was influenced by issues of race, class, and gender. In *Revolution and The Word*, Cathy Davidson argues that novels were particularly popular among the rising middle class in America because they addressed its concerns and portrayed some of its values; just as Richardson's fiction, argues Patricia Parker, brought the world of the middle class to the English novel (Parker 1986, 25). The sentimental novels written by William Hill Brown, Murray, Foster, Rowson, Tenney, Charles Brockden Brown, and Rebecca Rush appear to have been written for the white middle to upper classes. Since most sentimental novels during this period were dedicated to the "American fair," the target audience was the young, single woman grappling with one of the most pivotal issues of her life—marriage.

With the growth of interest in issues relating to privileged women during the early national period, the sentimental novel became an appropriate forum for the articulation of women's concerns or at least those concerns affecting the middle-class woman of the northeastern United States. Because Rowson, Foster, Murray, and Tenney set their scenes in New York, Connecticut, Massachusetts, and Pennsylvania, this study will focus upon issues—marriage, education, political rights— relating to young, single, white, middle- and upper-class women of the northeastern United States, although it will not ignore other race, class, and gender issues. Although many sentimental novels of the early nation used the seduction paradigm, this study will concentrate primarily upon Murray's *The Story of Margaretta* (1792), Rowson's *Charlotte Temple* (1794) and its sequel *Lucy Temple* (1828), Foster's *The Coquette* (1797) and *The Boarding School* (1798), and Tenney's *Female Quixotism*

---

produced over the years, the number of texts sold, and information provided by circulating library lists. In her profile on Susanna Rowson, Wendy Martin offers an overview of the publication history of *Charlotte Temple*. By 1805 *Charlotte Temple* had gone through sixteen editions. It has been suggested that *Charlotte Temple* was read by more than a million and a half novel readers by 1791 in England and by 1794 in America (Martin 1974, 1). In the *Dictionary of Literary Biography*, Davidson notes that Hannah Foster's *The Coquette* was considered the second best-selling novel before the nineteenth century (1985, 161). William Hill Brown's *The Power of Sympathy* also enjoyed a significant success during the late eighteenth century.

(1801). In effect, these novels, which either structure their plots around the seduction paradigm or incorporate narratives of seduction into the texts, do more than reflect the controversial debates over the status of middle-class women in the Northeast; they, in fact, comment upon them and propel them into new directions.

What, then, is so special about the narratives of seduction by these four writers? In *The Early American Novel*, Henri Petter notes that the seduction story was often considered a plot device calling for seducers to bear the brunt of the blame for corrupting innocence when, in fact, the young woman was often betrayed by her own weaknesses (1971, 257). Indeed, the seduction plot is more complex than this. Recent studies have resurrected seduction narratives from obscurity or from being considered pale imitations of Richardson's work by illuminating how the seduction story reflects woman's problematic status as the *Feme Covert* (a married or hidden woman whose rights are relinquished to her husband) and the *Feme Sole* (an unmarried woman) in the early nation. However, there has been no attempt to specifically link women's problematic status in America with the American Revolution's failure to free women from neocolonialist oppression. In addition, there has been no attempt to explore seduction as an euphemism for the most abusive means of maintaining women's allegiance to the new nation, nor has there been an attempt to explore seduction and rape as the ultimate representations of women's colonization in a rape culture—a culture that fosters violence against women and uses the fear of being victimized as a means of social control.

The narratives of seduction under review offer social critiques of the early nation and its colonial laws and customs, limited educational opportunities for women, and stereotypes of the fallen woman who was often viewed as a threat to the stability of the new republic. The seductions in *Charlotte Temple*, *The Coquette*, *Lucy Temple*, and *Female Quixotism* are more than formulaic fiction; they are, indeed, a complex signifying practice determined and reproduced by limited educational opportunities, colonial laws and customs, circumscribed roles for the middle-class woman, and the existence of a rape culture. While many narratives of seduction may be read as allegories of woman's sin in transgressing her prescribed role and her punishment in dying shortly after delivering the product of her transgression, these readings cannot be fully sustained in the novels under consideration, for they portray woman's fall as a consequence of a much greater social problem.

The social, political, and psychological issues of the works in question are portrayed within the frame of the sentimental novel, a genre that can also be examined as a compelling rhetorical device. In its most quintessential form, sentimentality is an outpouring of emotion, but it is also a term that is relative both to individual judgments and cultural change. The sentimental novel is a genre that appeals to the sympathy of readers, particularly during conventional seduction, death, or marriage scenes. This does not suggest, though, that the sentimental novel excludes or undermines the tragic. In the novels under consideration, the tragic and the sentimental work together to excite pity, fear, and terror. In a sense, there is a kinship between the sentimental novel and the Greek tragedy. In its most quintessential form, tragedy evokes both fear and pity; it can be instructive, cathartic, and therapeutic. The narrative strategy of storytelling incorporated into many sentimental novels can be instructive and cathartic as well. According to Jungian psychologist Clarissa Estes, storytelling has the potential to act as a balm to heal hurt minds; it is a form of instruction that guides the development of the listener's psyche as it conveys vital information about life (1992, 15). By transporting their audiences into realms in which people feared to tread, dramatists such as Sophocles, Aeschylus, and Euripides and sentimental novelists such as Rowson, Tenney, Foster, and Murray could impart vital information about confronting the complexities of life. However, sentimental novels acted out in private for the reader what the culture would not discuss in public or on the stage. In tragedy, lessons are taught by example, by tracing the fall of an individual. Like tragedy, the seduction narrative instructs by recounting the fall of a woman who steps beyond the periphery of her narrow world. Rather than having to confront supernatural forces or the demands of state, the sentimental heroine has to face the forces—social, political, psychological—that are particular to her world and give meaning to her everyday existence.

The narrative of seduction, though, was often the object of intense political debate and condemnation. During the late eighteenth century, Benjamin Rush, a leading proponent of female education, denounced novel reading upon the premise that novels were a licentious form of literature, the cause of female depravity, and the ultimate misrepresentation of American life ([1787] 1965, 31). For the middle-class woman of the late eighteenth century, however, the sentimental novel, particularly the narratives of seduction under review, did address her concerns of marriage, friendship, domesticity, education, and political rights.

Within the frame of sentimental literature, the narrators under consideration appeal to the sympathy and perhaps even empathy of their readers, but this appeal is a rhetorical device used to persuade readers to accept a particular point of view on an issue or at least to view an issue from another perspective. Rowson, for instance, was so committed to the drama created by the sentimental she entitled one chapter in *Charlotte Temple* "Which People Void of Feeling Need Not Read" ([1794] 1986, 112). The pathos elicited by the seductions of Charlotte Temple, Eliza Wharton, and Mary Lumley allows readers the imaginative space to reevaluate the stigmas attached to the fallen woman, the single mother, and the child born outside of marriage. This imaginative space allows the audience to consider decriminalizing premarital pregnancy by holding seducers accountable for their actions even when the legal systems did not. If rhetorically successful, the sentimental novel can elicit a response from its audience as evidenced by the prolific cult followings of *Charlotte Temple*, a novel that reached more than its intended audience by crossing race, class, and gender lines, or *The Coquette*, a novel purportedly based upon the seduction of an esteemed Connecticut woman named Elizabeth Whitman whose failure to disclose the identity of the father of her still-born child roused debate throughout the nineteenth century.[3]

Moreover, sensational seduction stories fascinated many American readers so much that they not only debated the paternity of Elizabeth Whitman's child, but they also journeyed to the Trinity Church cemetery in New York City to pay homage to the unmarked grave where Charlotte

---

3. Herbert Ross Brown notes that the Elizabeth Whitman scandal was well known throughout Connecticut (1940, 50). In the introduction to *The Coquette*, Cathy Davidson details the number of newspaper stories and sermons circulating in the United States about this tragedy. The enigmas surrounding this story were enough to inspire the creation of Charles Bolton's *The Elizabeth Whitman Mystery* (1912) and Caroline Dall's *The Romance of Association: or, One Last Glimpse of Charlotte Temple and Eliza Wharton* (1875) and for William Hill Brown to allude to it in his *The Power of Sympathy* (1969).

Temple was purportedly buried. Still, one wonders why novel readers were so intrigued by scandalous tales of seduction reenacted in novel after novel. Even the dramatist and educator Rowson, who was perhaps instrumental in perpetuating the seduction plot, remarked in *The Inquisitor*: "I wonder that novel readers are not tired of reading one story so many times with only the variation of its being told different ways" (1793, 3:189). To attest to the demand for seduction motifs, one eighteenth-century critic commented in the periodical the *Port Folio* that tales of seduction were to be found in

> by far the greater numbers of those novels, which crowd . . . a circulating library. They are sought out with such avidity, and run through with such delight by all those (a considerable part of my fellow citizens) who cannot resist the impulse of curiosity, or withstand the allurements of a title page. (Herbert Ross Brown [1802] 1940, 25)

If sentimental fiction is accepted as a genre that reveals vital information about a society, as Davidson and Tompkins argue, then there must have been something particularly telling during the late eighteenth century that touched many American readers to the point where tales of truth inspired the creation of their "torrid" literary counterparts. The sensational scandals of Elizabeth Whitman and Fanny Apthorp, a Massachusetts woman who committed suicide in 1788 rather than publicly reveal that her brother-in-law fathered her illegitimate child, provided the basis for novels such as The Power of Sympathy and *The Coquette* (Davidson 1986, 101). Perhaps because literature based upon sensational scandals was a relatively new phenomenon in America, readers were probing and inquisitive.

Seduction stories did more than just gratify the curious reader; they also served a variety of other functions. In addition to being a vital forum for political debate, seduction narratives offered some readers like Dorcasina Sheldon in *Female Quixotism* an escape from a mundane existence and the constricted realms of women. In a moment of reflection, Dorcasina reveals that she enjoys participating in the emotionalism created by novels and romances: "To read the suspense, the hope, the despair, the distraction, the interesting situations, the joy, the tumult,

and the bliss of faithful lovers . . . has been the delight of my life . . . "
(Tenney [1801] 1992, 221). As they titillated and forewarned, seduction
narratives offered readers the imaginative freedom to explore lives and
spheres that were often either out of their reach or the objects of intense
condemnation. As cautionary tales, novels like *Charlotte Temple, The
Coquette*, and their counterparts, argues Jan Lewis, are "not very subtle
warnings to young women without dowries that their value lay in their
virginity; if they would be sought after on the marriage market, they
must keep that commodity intact" (1987, 715).

On the other hand, Patricia McAlexander concludes that although
sentimental novels often promoted conservative values, they "in actuality promoted the ideal of passion in their readers. A feverish sense of the
titillating, semi-repressed sense of love, whether legal or illegal, spread
through America" (1975, 261). Indeed, the young, naive Charlotte
Temple and the more mature Eliza Wharton and Dorcasina Sheldon are
excited by passion as well as by handsome, charismatic men. While
these novels map the awakening of female desire, they map these desires
against the master narrative of Puritanism, and, of course, the clash
manifests itself within the texts. Perhaps this interest in passion and premarital relationships, whether legal or illegal, was a reflection of the
changing sexual mores of the age in which the bands of rigid Puritan
ethics loosened to the point where up to one-third of women in New
England delivered children less than nine months after their marriage
(Hindus 1975, 537).

While seduction tales may reflect a change in the sexual mores of the
late eighteenth century, they also may very well reflect a growing concern about violence against women. While comprehensive eighteenth-
century reader responses to novels like *Charlotte Temple, The Coquette*,
and *Female Quixotism* are unavailable, Janice Radway in *Reading The
Romance: Women, Patriarchy, and Popular Literature* offers some
insight about contemporary readings of romance novels that may be
quite applicable to understanding the female novel reader of the early
nation. Like the eighteenth-century narrative of seduction, many contemporary romance novels center upon women and include plots involv-
ing rape and seduction. Radway notes that in some contexts novels that
include rape and negative representations of men provide a space for some
female readers to explore their fears of dangerous men and threatening

situations, but, at the same time, exercise control over these fears with their own knowledge (1984, 140).

If the genre is effective, the reader of romance or seduction will sympathize, if not identify, with the heroine, even if the heroine has suffered and endured violation and rejection. Perhaps this identification with the heroine takes place not because the reader desires such an event to happen to her but because it offers a cathartic effect. Whether during the eighteenth or the twentieth century, violence against women pervades society. A female reader often understands the threat of violence in her culture and, thus, has internalized these fears. By identifying with the heroine, the reader can explore her own responses to these violations (ibid., 141).

The seduction genre certainly tapped into some very real fears in the new nation about the prevalence of violence against women. In a 1975 review of Susan Brownmiller's *Against Our Will: Men, Women and Rape*, Diane Johnson observes that "from a woman's earliest days she is attended by injunctions about strangers, warnings about dark streets, locks, escorts, and provocative behavior. She internalizes the lessons contained therein, that to break certain rules is to invite or deserve rape" (1975, 36). Certainly, a novel such as *The Coquette* contains warnings about provocative behavior that "invites" rape just as a novel like *Female Quixotism* contains representations of the dangers awaiting a woman who ventures forth into the night unescorted. In her exploration of rape and seduction in British fiction, Toni Reed suggests that the perpetuation of seduction motifs may be due in part to the fact that men historically and politically have always had the power to both subjugate and possess women. From a Jungian perspective, the conflict between the seducer and his victim could express "the collective oppression of women." The literature that represents this conflict also "represents a collective warning to women not to deviate from male-defined roles, for those who do are punished" (Reed 1988, 9). While the novels being explored do contain positive representations of men, they, for the most part, provide ample representations of villains that support the prevailing fears and warnings.

The prevalence of violence against women was not the concern of only the novelists in consideration; it was the concern of America's first lady, Abigail Adams. In a letter (20 April 1771) to her husband, Adams illuminates some of the conditions that prevent her countrywomen from traveling abroad unescorted:

> Women you know sir are considered domestic beings, and although they inherit an equal share of curiosity with the other sex, yet but few are hardy eno' to venture abroad, and explore the amazing variety of distant lands. The natural tenderness and delicacy of our constitutions, added to the many dangers we are subject to from your sex, renders it almost impossible for a single lady to travel without injury to her character. (Rossi 1973, 9)

While Adams certainly internalized some of the common myths about the frailty of women, she does relay two important insights: Women are taught to view men as the perpetrators of violence against women, and the fears of inviting danger and a damaged reputation are enough to keep women in docile, dependent, domestic positions. The seduction novel of the early nation voices and represents fears of rape, seduction, and sexual harassment not because these are fantasies on the part of the author or reader. Rather, seduction narratives explore the lives of characters who have suffered from these atrocities while providing readers with an imaginative space in which to suffer along with the heroine. In late eighteenth-century America, the seduction genre was appropriated by female writers for female audiences. Including the act of seduction and its consequences educated the young female reader about how to protect herself and how to control her own body. Given that novels written before 1820 reflected the mean age of females of the nation at twenty-five, the seduction novel, then, did speak to the young, middle- and upper-class northeastern woman (Davidson 1986, 112). Notwithstanding Benjamin Rush's stance that novels misrepresented the burgeoning nation, American life, as commented upon by Abigail Adams and others, did provide the material for sentimental fiction.

To counterattack condemnations of novel reading, many sentimental novelists adopted the convention of marketing their fiction as tales of truth. Novels by Charles Brockden Brown and William Hill Brown, contemporaries of Rowson, Foster, Murray, and Tenney, not only used the Richardsonian seduction paradigm but joined the debates over women's issues as well. *The Power of Sympathy* (1789) by William Hill

Brown was the first American sentimental novel to position itself as an educational story when it included a dedication reading: "To the young ladies of United Columbia, these volumes intended to represent the specious causes and to expose the fatal consequences of seduction; to inspire the female mind with a principle of self complacency . . . " ([1789] 1969, Preface). By positioning the seduction narrative as a vital educational tool, sentimental novelists could give their work an air of legitimacy in the face of heated political debates over the fatal effects of novel reading. Yet, in the preface of *Charlotte Temple*, Rowson proclaimed that rather than being a cause of female disorder and corruption, sentimental novels could be of service "to some who are so unfortunate as to have neither friends to advise, or understanding to direct them, through the various and unexpected evils that attend a young and unprotected woman in her first entrance into life" ([1794] 1986, 5). Indeed, many seduction novels published after 1789 in America were dedicated to the "American fair" for her better education.

Most certainly, seduction novels were strategically marketed as educational tools and advice literature for the young female reader, but they were also intricately connected to the emergence of the early nation by reflecting other fears, concerns, and conflicts that characterized the era. After the Revolution, America dubbed itself the new republic, a paradise regained. In this new Eden, many essayists, novelists, and politicians were concerned with the character America was to assume and project. Part of the success of this new character involved eliminating seducers, coquettes, and libertines from society because they were viewed as fatal to the success of the new nation. As a result of these concerns, the literature of the age assumed a particularly didactic tone as it instructed the nation's youth on morally acceptable roles and behavior. Of course, debates over the character of the new nation ranged from the conservative to the liberal, and this conflict manifested itself in the literature of the day.

In her exploration of virtue and seduction in the sentimental literature of the late eighteenth century, Jan Lewis concludes that seduction tales were not only cautionary advice to the young woman of the new republic but also political tracts that explored the potential for virtuous characters to exist in a corrupt and hostile world (1987, 716). Seduction stories hark back primarily to Genesis for their basic plot structure with, of course, Satan and Eve being the paradigms for the more secular and Americanized seducer and his prey; but Greek myth is also stocked with notorious womanizers, seducers, and rapists such as Zeus, Pan, and Silenus. Whether in Eden, ancient Greece, or America, the presence of stereotypical seducers and their victims set the stage for a reenactment of the Fall.

In the early nation, the daughters of Eve and the sons of Adam were seen to disrupt the very fabric of patriarchal structure, particularly when they did not heed the advice of their parents. Novelists such as Susanna Rowson, whose narrators often assume a particularly maternal role, attest to the importance of filial obedience for both sons and daughters; however, even Rowson points out in *Lucy Temple* as does Tabitha Tenney in *Female Quixotism* that the instruction given by some parents can be plagued with problems and ultimately mislead children down the path of misfortune or profligacy, as in the case of Mary Lumley of *Lucy Temple*. In other words, there are instances when failing to heed the advice of villainous or misinformed parents can be beneficial, as in the case of Dorcasina Sheldon of *Female Quixotism*. In her radical tract "On the Equality of the Sexes," the New England feminist, Judith Sargent Murray, dares to praise Eve for her disobedience or rather her bold step in eating from the forbidden tree because she was motivated by the loftiest desire—the desire for knowledge (1790, 225). In a sense, the novels of Rowson, Foster, Murray, and Tenney rewrite the Fall, but in the eighteenth-century version, the daughters of Eve are cast not as the cause of man's fall from grace but rather as victims of the social order which allows villainy to flourish. With rakes, seducers, and fortune hunters cast as counterparts to Satan in the new world, the seduction novel suggests, perhaps problematically, that to lead astray, prey upon the most helpless, and corrupt the innocent are inherent desires. The novels of these four authors work from the premise that the world is corrupt and virtue cannot flourish unless protected by wise counsel and supported with understanding.

Ann Douglas alludes to the connection between seduction narratives and the basic premise of the Adam and Eve story when she characterizes a novel like *Charlotte Temple* as a subliterate American myth that portrays a young, naive individual seduced by the hope and happiness associated with a new world and new land. Douglas further comments that the story of Charlotte Temple is also "the story of one girl's fate [translated] into the most compelling of tales, a passionate dramatization of the meaning of America, the 'subliterate myth' of the hopes and fears of those who came to its shores to find a new life" (1991, xv). John Adams, as well, viewed the tale of seduction as particularly pertinent to the new republic when he saw Americans, unschooled in the ways of the world, tempted by the hope of democracy, an experimental form of government. In essence, Americans were implementing what had been only theorized by European Enlightenment thinkers such as Rousseau, Locke, and Hobbes.

The success of seduction narratives in America may be dependent upon additional issues and concerns that reach back farther than the revolutionary era to America's colonial heritage. From the vantage points of Puritanism and Calvinism, seduction tales can be read conservatively. It is apropos that an area of the country steeped in Puritanism and Calvinism should be intrigued with representations of sin and punishment in the seduction genre. Puritanism and Calvinism stressed the importance of social order, particularly hierarchical order with God as the center and head of the universe, and the human father on earth as the head of family and state (Koehler 1980, 22). Obedient individuals were expected to maintain their biologically determined gender roles, and if they overstepped their roles, they were expected to be punished as Hester Prynne was punished in Hawthorne's *The Scarlet Letter* (1850) for the sexual transgression of adultery. The Puritan Cotton Mather often cautioned his congregation that premarital or extramarital sex would destroy a transgressor's body and mind, and even worse his or her chances for salvation (ibid., 73). For those schooled in Puritan and Calvinist beliefs, life was a moral trial. All the heroines in the seduction novels under review not only endure their fates heroically, but they also suffer as the Puritan script dictated.

It became a cultural imperative for the daughters of Eve and the Puritan heritage to suffer or even die from sexual transgressions, and this is certainly an understandable reason for Nina Baym calling seduction novels "demoralized literature" in *Woman's Fiction* (1978, 51). Perhaps the demise of so many transgressive heroines in the seduction genre may be attributed to the lack of appropriate cultural space for them to occupy. What was America to do with transgressive women? Where could the transgressive woman dwell in dignity rather than shame? For Hester Prynne, it was on the margins of town. For Eliza Wharton, it was at a wayside tavern in Danvers, Massachusetts. As transgressive women, Eliza Wharton, Charlotte Temple, Mary Lumley, Frances Wellwood, and their counterparts are dispossessed women; they belong to neither father nor husband. Because the transgressive woman was believed to disrupt the very fabric of social hierarchy, she was expected to be punished and held up as a moral lesson, just as was Elizabeth Whitman, the prototype for *The Coquette*, in newspapers and church sermons. Whitman was purported to have been misled not only by novel reading but also by aspiring beyond her middle-class status and ultimately questioning Calvinist predestination. As Cathy Davidson points out in *Revolution and The Word*, Whitman's story was read mainly by those who wanted to superimpose their own meaning onto her life (1986, 142). While the novels of Foster, Murray, Tenney, and Rowson embody the master narratives of Genesis, Puritanism, and Calvinism, they also work to displace their legitimacy by dismantling the traditional ways of viewing "fallen" women and the reasons for their conventional deaths within the seduction paradigm.

The transgressions of Charlotte Temple, Eliza Wharton, Mary Lumley, Dorcasina Sheldon, and Frances Wellwood are committed, in part, out of frustration or dissatisfaction with their lot and, in part, out of the failure of their prescribed lot to prepare them to deal with rogues and fortune hunters. For those in positions of authority, using the transgressive woman as a scapegoat is far more convenient than addressing the much greater social problems that foster the demise of young women who are ultimately portrayed by many writers as martyrs rather than sinners. The sentimental novels in question reflect many aspects of their culture, including the shift in views not only about the status of middle- and upper-class women but about transgressive women in the new republic. During the seventeenth century, the Puritan minister John Cotton preached the view, embraced by many individuals, that whether a woman engaged freely in premarital sex or was raped, she was still a whore (Koehler 1980, 74). This conviction persisted throughout the eighteenth century. As the turn of the century approached, this view began to wane with some people. There were certainly individuals like Lydia Maria Child who, in *The Mother's Book* (1831), would not recommend *Charlotte*

Temple for young girls because she thought it would lead them astray. Nonetheless, there was a growing body of literature portraying the fallen woman sympathetically. Of course, Susanna Rowson's novels were among this literature. Dorothy Weil notes that Rowson's championship of the fallen woman is a central part of her plea for the transformation of society's conventional attitudes toward women (1976, 62).

Being the utterly subservient, passive recipient of a husband's and a father's rule was no longer acceptable for many women. Novelist Tenney, educator Rowson, and theorist Murray were not the only women in New England who desired to transform power relations between men and women and carve out new roles for women. Eliza Southgate, diarist and student at Rowson's Female Academy in Medford, Massachusetts, revealed her views of republican daughters and their embracing of republican ideologies—the rights to life, liberty, and the pursuit of happiness—in numerous letters to family and friends. America's first lady Abigail Adams also championed women's rights in laws and education in her correspondence to family and friends. A frequent recipient of Abigail Adams' celebrated letters was her dear friend Mercy Warren, whose notable contributions to society went far beyond being the first female dramatist to write propaganda pieces in support of the patriotic cause. Adams and Warren, both of whom shared if not influenced Judith Sargent Murray's theories, believed gender determined women's subordinate status in society; this, they felt, prevented women from tasting the fruits of higher education and civil life enjoyed by men of their race and class. The characteristics that were often espoused and expected of women—passivity, silence, obedience—were the exact characteristics that confined women within the walls of domesticity. For Murray, Tenney, and Rowson, these characteristics contributed to a young woman's inability to resist plotting, manipulative profligates who might very well scheme their way into her home. While scholars still debate whether the American Revolution significantly changed the legal status of women, the war for independence did stir a rise in feminist consciousness. This, though, should not be viewed as unusual or coincidental; lest we forget, America, too, is a transgressive woman who fought her mother country for life, liberty, and the pursuit of happiness—for the ability to grow up and leave the state of perpetual childhood.

Of all the literary, cultural, and political factors that culminated in novels such as *Charlotte Temple, The Coquette, The Story of Margaretta,* and *Female Quixotism,* the one element that proves to be the most controversial, intriguing, and, of course, essential to the paradigm is seduction. The term seduction is ambiguous because it can assume a multiplicity of meanings for different people in different contexts. Therefore, an understanding of the term seduction, how it fits into a cultural and political context of the early nation, and how it serves as a metaphor for women's colonized status in the new republic is necessary.

In *Seductions: Studies in Reading and Culture,* Jane Miller explores various meanings of seduction which range from both the dangerous and delightful to the resistible and irresistible (1991, 2). Seduction, as explained by Miller, may be thought of not only as a metaphor, but also as a "means by which sexual relations can be inserted into any understanding of how power is experienced in societies built on inequality" (ibid.). Some may argue that seduction differs from rape, and although at times seduction may appear as or be renamed rape, the issue of consent quite necessarily separates the two. However, seduction, particularly in the novels under review, involves the victim being deliberately misled or manipulated into consenting under false promises.

According to *Webster's Ninth New Collegiate Dictionary,* seduction is the enticement of an individual to unlawful sexual intercourse or the deliberate leading astray of an individual by persuasion or false promises (1984, 1062). According to earlier dictionaries, an eighteenth-century American would have accepted this as a definition as well. When theorists, critics, and readers refuse to view seduction as a form of rape, they fail to understand the history or context of rape and seduction. To understand seduction as rape, we must understand that many a rape or seduction is brought about by lies, psychological intimidation, and false pretenses. Susan Brownmiller argues that historically the term seduction has been differentiated from rape because seduction did not necessarily involve the use or threat of physical force, often the criterion that defines rape for many. In actuality, coercion assumes many forms, from the economic to the emotional, and "the imposition of sex by an authority figure," concludes Brownmiller, "is hardly consensual or 'equal'" (1975, 271).

Mackinnon: it never is.

In *Seduction and Theory*, Martha Noel Evans similarly proposes that seduction implies, if not overtly denotes, "the use of persuasion in the sexual corruption of another individual" (1989, 74). Although Evans' essay discusses Freud's use of the term seduction as an euphemism for incest, her examination of the term's misuse is particularly pertinent to understanding the misleading substitution of the term seduction for rape in late eighteenth-century sentimental fiction. Evans notes that "The shift in Freud's vocabulary from words denoting injury to one implying persuasion and even possible assent can be seen as part of a widespread social pattern which minimizes the sexual exploitation of women by men" (ibid.). When the patriarchy holds a woman accountable for a man's sexual choices, actions, and crimes, it can minimize if not mask the widespread abuse of patriarchal power.

While seduction novels have been understandably labeled novels of victimization, the novels under review explore the cultural and political sources and mechanisms that keep women passive sexual prey. These novels serve as loci for the exploration of victimization and self-affirmation. Revealing the forces that act upon women provides an education that cannot be taught at the local schoolhouse or academy. In effect, the novels under consideration offer alternative insights on the genre's stereotypical representation of women by juxtaposing fallen women to women who do escape the cunning of a seducer. A young woman's ability or failure to resist the wiles of a seducer is often linked to her education and socialization. Education and socialization become the keys to understanding the means by which seduction as a social practice is reproduced in novel after novel.

While authorial intentionality is certainly difficult to assess, many early American sentimental novelists clearly position their novels as educational tools: a forewarning, in part, to the young, middle-class single woman that even Eden had a villain and that he may appear in the guise of a handsome, charismatic man or as various facets of the social order in which she dwells. Most appropriately, Cathy Davidson in *Revolution and The Word* concludes that the narrative of seduction became the best form of birth control available to the privileged woman (1986, 116). In other words, if a young woman can understand the mechanisms that allow seduction as a practice to reproduce itself over and over, then perhaps she could break the perpetuation of the cycle.

Within the novels under consideration, a young woman's ability or failure to resist seduction is contingent, in part, upon the kind of education
and socialization she receives. Often, middle-class girls were encouraged
to study reading, writing, religion, and sewing. Middle- and upper-class
women could attend private academies or finishing schools, but the curricula focused upon preparing young women to be good wives and mothers. While being prepared for civic life, young men of the same race and
class could expect to study geography, history, and science. With a few
exceptions, the poor and most African Americans did not have access to
local schools or, in many cases, even basic literacy. For the most part,
the subjects traditionally taught to females at the local schoolhouse or
private academy would not seriously develop their intellect or critical-
thinking skills—the skills necessary to encourage women to exercise
sound judgment in life choices. The authors of both *Charlotte Temple*
and *Female Quixotism* note in their prefaces that the heroines suffer
from the fatal effects of seduction because their education did not develop their critical skills; thus, these heroines were not able to detect seduction and avoid its consequences. Ultimately, the kind of education both
males and females might have received during the early national period
was determined by the central culture's practice of neocolonialism. In
other words, the very rights that the patriots fought for during the
Revolution were in turn systematically denied to many Americans. As
Jean Baker Miller explains, the ruling power of a culture has the greatest
influence in determining a culture's outlook, ideologies, and social practices (1976, 8).

   In *The Empire Writes Back*, Bill Ashcroft, Gareth Griffiths, and
Helen Tiffin provide a reminder that America is not only a colonized land
but a land that participates in neocolonization (1989, 16). When the
patriots ignited a revolution against England, they challenged their
mother country's world view and way of ordering reality; they asserted
their fundamental differences with a country that denied them voice,
representation, and self-determination; and they struggled against their
mother country because they desired a new nation and identity founded
upon freedom, security, self-government, and the pursuit of happiness.
However, once the patriots achieved their victory over England, they, in
turn, used the very practices they had fought to free themselves of
against other Americans, particularly women.

Both Gayatri Spivak and Nancy Hartsock inscribe gender into the power relations between the colonized and the colonizer. These scholars explain that women as the colonized Other are often kept in their prescribed place through fear, coercion, force, and violence. For all practical purposes, women are legally and politically invisible. If the colonized woman is legally defined as property, she cannot contribute to official history or culture. Represented as biologically and intellectually inferior, women are encouraged to develop only characteristics pleasing to those in a dominant position. If the colonized woman is anything but silent, docile, submissive, and compliant, the patriarchy views her as disruptive, and thus controls her through force, coercion, and violence, which become legitimized and necessary to maintain social and political order for the greater good. Influenced by the philosophy of colonialism, the patriarchy legitimizes and naturalizes inequality in laws, sexual politics, dominant ideologies, and social practices. If America's founding fathers were to be father to a nation, then they were to be the head of state and family; their assumed moral superiority dictated the ways of viewing and making sense of reality.

After the Revolution, America's founding fathers conveniently maintained English colonial laws regarding women in the new republic. Abigail Adams' noted plea for her husband to "Remember the Ladies" (March 31, 1776) in the new laws that were to set a nation in motion attests to the fact that women's concerns were ignored:

> I desire you [John Adams] would Remember the Ladies, and be more generous and favorable to them than your ancestors. Do not put such unlimited power into the hands of husbands. Remember all men would be tyrants if they could. If particular care and attention is not paid to the ladies we are determined to ferment a rebellion, and will not hold ourselves bound by any laws in which we have no voice, or representation. (Rossi 1973, 10–11)

Insightful and revealing, this plea to change the course of history and reevaluate the legal prerogatives of husbands was deliberately and systematically rejected by John Adams:

As to your extraordinary code of laws, I cannot but laugh. We
have been told that our struggle has loosened the bands of government everywhere. That children and apprentices were disobedient—that schools and colleges were grown turbulent—that
Indians slighted their guardians and Negroes grew insolent to
their masters. But your letter was the first intimation that another tribe more numerous and powerful than all the rest were
grown discontented. Depend upon it, we know better than repeal
our masculine system. (ibid.,11)

John Adams spurns Abigail's plea to reevaluate the legal rights of husbands and wives, but he also reveals that the Revolutionary War in which
patriot wives and daughters were called to participate for the greater
good was not fought for them, nor was it fought for African or Native
Americans. In the creation of a new set of *post-revolutionary* laws, a
woman's colonized status was legitimized with systematic calculation.

In addition to neocolonialist practices in education, laws, and customs, seduction is also fostered by the presence of a rape culture. One of
the many insights Susan Brownmiller offers in *Against Our Will: Men,
Women and Rape* is that instances of sexual harassment, rape, and
attempted rape were recorded during colonial America and the early
republic. (1975, 115) In particular, the patriots gathered evidence of
these crimes to help support the revolutionary cause in America; these
crimes were additional examples of how Americans were being terror-
ized and denied their rights to freedom, happiness, and security. The
gathering of this evidence by the patriots, though, was not a way of
"remembering the ladies." As noted by Brownmiller, Rus Funk, Angela
Davis, John Stoltenberg, and a variety of other scholars, rape and sexual
harassment were crimes against the male estate. The novels by Rowson,
Murray, Tenney, and Foster represent the continued existence of rape
and seduction well after the Revolution during a period when women
were still legally defined as property. However, these late eighteenth-century novels note that rape was not committed solely by the British as a
means of colonialist terrorism against the male American estate. Rather,
rape was being committed also by Americans upon other Americans as the
ultimate reenactment of the relationship between colonizer and colonized.

Since Richardson's Lovelace is the prototype for many of the seducers portrayed in sentimental novels, an understanding is needed of his view of Clarissa and how this view is shaped by a rapist and colonialist attitude. In a letter to his friend John Belford, Lovelace explains that there are three passions that navigate his life and his rape of Clarissa: "I have three passions that sway me by turns; all imperial ones. Love, revenge, ambition, or a desire of conquest" (Richardson [1747/8] 1962, 261). From the vantage point of an imperialist, Lovelace rapes a woman whom he actually places on the level of the ethereal. Clarissa is a pure, angelic body, an unconquered land that Lovelace desires to subdue and possess. Ultimately, the female body serves as the site for the reenactment of imperial desires. From an imperialist perspective, Lovelace openly admits that he "prefers the pursuit and conquest of a fine woman to all the joys of life" (ibid., 210). Within the context of *Clarissa* and the narratives of seduction in question, rape or seduction assumes a colonialist or neocolonialist strategy; rape or seduction is a reenactment of colonialist endeavors. Ultimately, *Clarissa* and the narratives of seduction under review point to the existence of what John Stoltenberg terms a "rapist ethic," which is intricately connected to neocolonialism.

In *Refusing To Be A Man*, Stoltenberg explains that a "rapist ethic" is a system of attaching value to conduct that men learn during their sexual identity socialization. Part of this socialization entails reaffirming man's egocentrism and his power over others, particularly women. Integral to a "rapist ethic" and to the male sexual identity is the reversal of accountability; that is, in a "rapist ethic," a rapist would often fail to accept personal responsibility for an act of rape by blaming the victim of the act as solely responsible. From an acute psychological perspective, Stoltenberg concludes that this is a form of projection, "of seeing one's wrong in the person one is wronging, which is the same as saying that one has done no wrong" (1990, 19). As scheming, manipulative, and vengeful, Lovelace and his counterparts in American sentimental novels epitomize the rapist, colonizer mentality, and their innocent prey provides the body they can access, possess, subdue, and conquer.

To help illuminate seduction as a complex signifying practice that is reproduced both in eighteenth-century novels and in early American society, I employ feminist theory, postcolonial theory and cultural studies. In particular, the writings of Bill Ashcroft, Gareth Griffiths, Helen

Tiffin, Susan Brownmiller, John Stoltenberg, Rus Funk, Nancy Cott, Linda Kerber, and Cathy Davidson provide my primary methodological and theoretical bases. The following chapters develop more fully the conditions that allow seduction as a social practice to reproduce itself.

The first chapter explores the connection between a young woman's education and socialization and her ability or failure to resist the artifice of a seducer. In particular, the seduction novels under consideration illustrate the consequences of conventional education and socialization practices that fail to develop a woman's critical-thinking skills—the skills necessary to detect seducers. In addition, this chapter examines Murray's feminist essays on independence and education and Susanna Rowson's pioneering contributions as an educator, textbook writer, and founder of an academy for women.

The second chapter draws a link between seduction and the privileged woman's limited status and role in the early nation as defined by laws and customs. In addition, this chapter discusses how these novels expose the double standard in the early nation, as well as the early nation's failure to extend unalienable rights to women.

The third chapter investigates the fostering of rape, seduction, and sexual harassment in a rape culture. Particular attention is given to analyzing the "rapist ethic" as defined by John Stoltenberg, seduction as a reenactment of the relationship between colonizer and colonized, the psychological ramifications of seduction, and conventional conclusions in the seduction genre.

The conclusion illuminates the contributions that Murray, Rowson, Foster, and Tenney have made to American literature and the origins of the women's movement. Most certainly, many of the themes explored in the novels of Rowson, Foster, Murray, and Tenney were reexamined and further developed in nineteenth and twentieth-century novels. Whether as novelists, teachers, or educational theorists, these four women also contributed to an emergent feminist consciousness in the new nation by illuminating rape, sexual harassment, the double standard, and violence against women as compelling social problems. Indeed, the tales of Charlotte Temple, Mary Lumley, Eliza Wharton, Dorcasina Sheldon, and Frances Wellwood are still, in many ways, tales of truth for the twentieth-century woman.

1
Intervening Before the Fall:
Re-educating the "American Fair"

IN THE SUMMER of 1778, Abigail Adams came to the defense of her countrywomen yet again when she passionately reminded her husband of the insufficient state of female education and the current trends forming to thwart advancement in female accomplishment: "[In] this country you need not be told how much female education is neglected, nor how fashionable it has been to ridicule female learning" (Cott 1977, 106). During the late eighteenth century, Abigail Adams was one of a growing number of women who demanded that the rights for which the patriots fought during the Revolution be extended to women, particularly in the realm of education. Indeed, some of the most turbulent debates of the early nation centered upon educational reform for both men and women, and, most curiously, the seduction novels commented upon those debates and propelled them in new directions.

In their narratives of seduction, Rowson, Murray, Foster, and Tenney joined the controversy over female learning with great vigor when they called for the reevaluation of conventional educational programs for girls and young women concomitant to the ongoing restructuring of conventional education for boys and young men. In particular, the novels under review express an alarming concern over the link between insufficient education and seduction. Thus, the seduction narrative provides not only a forum for these novelists to discuss their perspectives on educational reform for the women of their race and class but also an illustration of seduction as a practice determined, in part, by limited or deficient educational opportunities.

Although *Charlotte Temple*, *Female Quixotism*, *The Boarding School*, and *The Story of Margaretta* all enter the debate over educational reform, they address the debate from various vantage points. As educational theorists, both Murray and Foster directly raise the issue of curriculum reform by proposing their own learning regimens within their novels. On the other hand, Rowson's most detailed calls for changes in the traditional curricula for privileged women are found not in her novels but in her creation of innovative textbooks and their use at her esteemed private academy for young women in Massachusetts. In her novels, Rowson appears to be most concerned with exploring the consequences some young women must endure when they are ill-educated to deal with a hostile world. In her profile on Rowson, Wendy Martin notes that Rowson's Biblical interests pervade all her novels; *Charlotte Temple* and its sequel assume a particularly moralistic tone, which positions the novels as sermons and warnings (1974, 4). The adoption of a sermonic tone provides Rowson with another medium to impart vital information about the complexity of life to young women. *Female Quixotism* also positions itself as a guide that provides instruction to the young women of the early nation; however, it also parodies some of the controversies surrounding novel reading and indirectly debates the question of who suffers the most from a deficient or misguided education—men or women.

Among the novelists, Rowson is the first to establish a causal relationship between seduction and the deficient state of education for women during the late eighteenth century. For Rowson, Murray, and Foster, a deficient education has the potential to lead to a variety of consequences, one of which is seduction. Once a young woman is trapped in the causal chain of events dictated by the seduction paradigm, the resolution, according to the cultural imperative of the age, is either ostracism or the death of the fallen woman. Although Rowson, Foster, Murray, and Tenney map out these cultural imperatives, their novels are also indicative of changing perspectives. The novels act as preventative medicine by illustrating not only the chain of events that often results when a young woman is seduced, but also that this sequence of events— seduction, pregnancy, abandonment, death—need not result if a young woman possesses the necessary critical-thinking skills and a knowledge of human behavior. As the colonized Other, a woman traditionally would not have been encouraged to develop these critical capacities. Since the policy makers of the early nation often viewed women in essentially utilitarian terms, women's needs or concerns were considered secondary to those of their husbands and sons—the nation.

The seduction novels by Rowson and her New England contemporaries not only challenge Puritan and colonialist perspectives on education but also ask who possesses the right to determine the kind of education girls and women should have available within the home, the local schoolhouse, and the private academy. In the preface of *Charlotte Temple*, the narrator, like many narrators of the late eighteenth century, defends her right to publish her novel on the conventional basis that she is educating young readers. "If the following tale should save one hapless fair from the errors which ruined poor Charlotte," dramatically proclaims Rowson in her preface, "I shall feel a much higher gratification in reflecting on this trifling performance, than could possibly result from the applause which might attend . . . literature whose tendency might deprave the heart or mislead the understanding" ([1794] 1986, 6). Quite aware of the power of literature to influence readers, Rowson makes her own readers and critics cognizant of her contention that although some of the finest pieces of literature may mislead readers, she has produced a piece that promotes what she considers to be the happiness and security of females.

In fact, Rowson's declaration becomes more than just a conventional device, for it actively seeks to empower young women with information that encourages them to assume an active rather than a passive role in the prevention of seduction. In particular, the author of *Charlotte Temple* is interested in tracing the sequence of events experienced by young women "spoilt by a mistaken education" and " . . . thrown on an unfeeling world without the least power to defend themselves from the snares not only of the other sex, but from the more dangerous arts of the profligate of their own" (ibid., 5). The story of a young girl unable to defend herself in a hostile world is the story of Charlotte, but the underlying assumption in the preface is that this is the story of more than just one young woman. This also becomes the story of Mary Lumley, Alice Lonsdale, Frances Wellwood, and the many young women met in numerous narratives of seduction published during the early national period.

The narrator's preface to *Charlotte Temple* provides the only direct acknowledgment of a correlation between the insufficient education of young women and seduction. The story of the fifteen-year-old Charlotte then becomes a demonstration of a young girl's inability to cope with a world outside her home. More importantly, the novel illustrates the inability of youth, naivete, docility, and obedience to overcome the arts of persuasion, cunning, and manipulation demonstrated by men such as Lieutenant Montraville and Officer Belcour or a woman such as Mademoiselle La Rue. Part of Charlotte's inability to prevent her seduction can be traced to the opening chapter, "A Boarding School," the place near the locale she first met her seducer. Although Rowson does draw a direct parallel between the mistaken education Charlotte received at her school in England and her inability to escape the snares of Montraville and La Rue, she does not provide any additional information about the particulars of Charlotte's learning and why it is "mistaken." What, then, constitutes this "mistaken education" alluded to by Rowson?

At this early point in American history, education was neither a right available to all Americans nor a systematic program available in all towns. In her introduction to Murray's *The Gleaner*, Nina Baym notes that, before the American Revolution, there were minimal educational opportunities opened to women in general (1992, v). For some white middle- and upper-class females there were some "dame schools" or finishing schools available, such as the school presumably attended by the heroine of *Charlotte Temple*. Although there are exceptions, many white working-class and African and Native Americans did not have access to local schoolhouses for a variety of reasons. Some could not be spared from contributing to their family's economic security; their services were needed on the farm or in household production. Finances also prevented many girls and boys from receiving private tutorial lessons or an education at an academy or college.[1] Indeed, college and university education was available only for middle and upper-class young men. In many areas of America, African Americans were legally prevented from attaining even basic literacy; and if many southern states did not make teaching slaves illegal, custom often discouraged them from formal learning.[2] There were exceptions, though. Phillis Wheatley, a slave purchased by a

1.   Colleges and universities were closed to women until the opening of Oberlin in 1837.

2.   Paula Rothenberg states that a North Carolina law was typical of the laws preventing the education of slaves throughout the United States. While this law did not go into effect until the 1830s, its sentiments were certainly implemented

bizarre reference

Boston family in 1761, was encouraged to study writing, poetry, Latin, literature, and mythology (Woody 1966, 132). In *Women, Race and Class*, Angela Davis provides a detailed discussion of the struggle for black men and women to gain access to public and private education during this period in Boston and other areas of the country (1983, 98–102).

During the late eighteenth century, more schools opened for females, although primarily those of the middle- to upper- class. While opening more such schools might appear to be a liberating measure, it may very well have been, in some instances, part of a conservative agenda to keep women bound to the home and hearth. For instance, even though the Boston Act of 1789 designated that girls and boys be taught the same subject matter—reading, writing, and arithmetic—in public schools, girls still attended school fewer hours per week and fewer months per year (Woody 1966, 146). A few years earlier, a Massachusetts man, John Eliot, informed his friend Jeremy Belknap about the Boston school district's curtailing the elementary education of girls:

> We don't pretend to teach . . . female[s] . . . anything more than dancing, or a little music perhaps, (and these accomplishments must necessarily be confined to a very few,) except [for] private schools for writing, which enables them to write a copy, sign their names . . . which they might not be able to do without such a privilege. (ibid., 145–46)

Although some schools were open to girls in 1782, they were opened for a conservative agenda and in some instances with far more contempt than enthusiasm. Not until 1828 did Boston allow girls to attend school year round (ibid., 146).

Clearly, race, class, and gender issues determined levels of education available to males and females of the early nation. The ability of Eliot

---

years before. "An Act to Prevent All Persons from Teaching Slaves to Read or Write, the Use of Figures Excepted" issued by North Carolina in 1830–1831 stated: "...the teaching of slaves to read and write, has a tendency to excite dissatisfaction in their minds, and to produce insurrection and rebellion, to manifest injury of the citizens of this state" (Rothenberg 1992, 265).

and his cohorts to favor their characteristics and world views over others reflected the neocolonialist philosophies implemented by legislators. Limited educational opportunities for women ensured women's status as the weaker sex and the status of husbands as the heads of family and state. Inequality in formal and informal education provided another means of institutionalizing the naturalization of constructed differences between men and women of different races and classes.

Although the subject matter taught to girls and young women at the schoolhouse and private academy often varied, it was still largely determined by gender. Many female academies were synonymous with finishing schools; their programs were designed to prepare young women to be good wives and mothers. Concomitantly, middle- and upper-class boys and young men were reared for college and civic life. In *The Bonds of Womanhood*, Nancy Cott notes that the main argument used to support the education of girls and young women at home, in local schoolhouses, or at private academies was purely utilitarian (1977, 108). While the education of both men and women after the Revolution was embedded in utility and practicality, girls were still educated in relationship to men; boys and young men were educated in relationship to the state. While middle- and upper-class girls were often taught little beyond remedial mathematics and writing, religion and sewing, young men of the same race and class could study rhetoric, science, geometry, and philosophy as their tutors prepared them for college. For the most part, programs varied from school to school just as perspectives on female learning varied from person to person.

Indeed, stigmas attached to female learning prevented many females from receiving an education beyond reading and writing. The predominant arguments of the age maintained that education beyond reading, writing, and arithmetic would encourage unruly behavior and psychological illness in females. Further, female learning might disrupt the conviction embraced by philosophers, politicians, and religious zealots that the universe was male-centered. Linda Kerber in "Daughters of Columbia: Educating Women for the Republic" reminds her audience that the intellectual milieu of the eighteenth century often equated female learning with pedantry and masculinity (1987, 107). Jean Baker Miller argues that often when women as subordinates "assume that their own needs have equal validity and proceed to explore and state them more openly, they will be seen as creating conflict" (1976, 17). In these particular instances, a woman as subordinate or as colonized Other is seen as inviting conflict because her desire for learning disrupts gender roles and social organization. A woman's desire for learning beyond elementary education also invites the stereotypes of masculine-mannered women and "blue stockings" (a blue stocking refers to a woman having intellectual or literary interests). Of course, nineteenth-century writers such as Sara Willis Parton (Fanny Fern), Catherine Sedgwick, and Louisa May Alcott grappled with the stigmas associated with female learning and female writers well after Abigail Adams voiced her concern about the fashionable trends of ridiculing the education of women.

Shifts in the traditional view of the privileged woman's education began to emerge concomitant to Benjamin Rush's public call to revamp the curricula for girls. In "Thoughts Upon Female Education" (1787), Rush put forth his justification for a more evolved educational agenda that included science, history, and mathematics.[3] However, he supported female learning as part of a conservative agenda as clearly illustrated in the rationale he offers to his gentlemen friends: "If men believe that ignorance is favorable to the government of the female sex, they are certainly deceived, for a weak and ignorant woman will always be governed with the greatest difficulty" ([1787] 1965, 39). Even as he perpetuated the myths that women are naturally unruly and disobedient, Rush attempted to quell the fears of men who felt that female learning was tantamount to the overthrow of male power. Ultimately, Rush was not calling for the adoption of female equality in education, nor was he calling for the adoption of Murray's concept of egalitarian feminism articulated in her essays. Like her friend Mercy Warren, Murray fervently believed in the natural equality of the sexes. In "Sentiments on Education" (1789), Murray passionately contends that "the sexes are congenial; they are copyists of each other; and their opinions and habits are elevated or degraded . . . by the same circumstances" (707). In contrast, representing a neocolonialist perspective, Rush believed that education would

---

3.   "Thoughts Upon Female Education" was originally delivered to family, friends, and visitors of the Young Ladies' Academy in Philadelphia (July 28, 1787). Rush was one of the academy's trustees.

allow women to better understand their roles as obedient, submissive wives and daughters; education could be a vital tool in further silencing and marginalizing women. Ultimately, many of the growing number of female academies in the early nation did not have the benefit of Rowson's pioneering educational agenda or textbooks, or the kind of education advocated in Foster's *The Boarding School*, or even the benefit of the well-rounded curriculum recommended by Murray in her essays and novel.

Since his speech to the academy predates the publication of the first novels written by American women during the early national period, Rush could not have foreseen that the two leading female advocates of women's educational reform—Murray and Rowson—would within a few years of his speech publish their own novels and cast them as educational texts. Moreover, Rush could not have anticipated the contributions that Murray and Rowson would make as educational theorists and instructors. While Rush's curricula for young women may appear quite conservative to the contemporary reader, educating women beyond basic reading and writing was indeed a controversial issue. Just the inclusion of mathematics or bookkeeping was enough to stir fierce debate.

While the egalitarian feminist Murray did share some of Rush's views on revising traditional educational practices for women, she did not share his rationale supporting curriculum reform. Murray is most noted in American history, literature, and culture for her profound essays debunking myths of gender and supporting women's natural equality to men, but her radical convictions and literary talents also manifested themselves in other genres. In addition to being a dramatist, Murray was a sentimental novelist who capitalized on one of the most fashionable motifs in late eighteenth-century American literature—seduction. Vena Bernadette Field, Murray's biographer, explains that *The Story of Margaretta* (1792, 1798) acts as a "mouthpiece for the expression of her own opinions on manners, education, and other social matters" (1931, 54).[4] While she certainly employed the novel as a forum for her beliefs,

---

4.   In the introduction to the 1992 edition of *The Gleaner*, Nina Baym notes that 759 individuals subscribed to 825 sets of Murray's collection (8). Vena Bernadette Field also notes that the subscription list for *The Gleaner* attracted influential buyers, including George and Martha Washington, Mercy and James

perhaps as Rowson used her novel to educate and inform young women, Murray, like Rowson and Foster, also used the novel to establish a link between deficient education and seduction. Murray believed that a well-rounded education was the answer, at least in part, to women's survival in the new republic; a young woman's ability or failure to resist the wiles of a seducer was contingent upon the kind of education she received.

Understanding the literary and political milieu of her day, Murray strives, like many of her contemporaries, to justify novel reading before explaining the attempted seduction of Margaretta and the importance of women's education. The history of Margaretta is primarily related by the narrator of the story, Mr. Vigillius, an essayist for the *Massachusetts Magazine* and the foster parent of Margaretta. Within the course of his essay writing, in which he reports upon the activities, education, and marriage of Margaretta, Vigillius receives a number of letters from readers who want to learn more about his adopted daughter. In one letter, a reader suggests that the essayist hesitates to paint a broader picture of the esteemed Margaretta because he is fearful of being labeled a novelist.

While the story includes some of the common literary and cultural assumptions about novels and novel reading—an issue later parodied in Tenney's *Female Quixotism* (1801)—it does provide strong arguments in support of novelists. Essay writing, proclaims one letter writer to Vigillius, is of the highest excellence, but novels could also be "productive of the highest utility," a belief also embraced by Rowson (Murray [1797] 1992, 49). At this point, Murray's novel documents the shift in the controversy so politicized in the new republic. Vigillius claims that if an author is sincere with amiable intentions, then the novel may be of service to many readers (ibid., 49). In fact, other letters written to the columnist request a more detailed portrait of Margaretta. A novel about Margaretta would offer young women advice on how to shape their future conduct—a topic found not only in the *Massachusetts Magazine* but

Warren, writer Sarah Morton, Governor John Taylor Gilman of New Hampshire, General Henry Knox, and many other notable Americans (1931, 43).

Murray's *Story of Margaretta* was initially published in her monthly column for the *Massachusetts Magazine* (called "The Gleaner" in 1792). Once the magazine dissolved, Murray could not finish the installments in periodical form. Later in the three volume collection of her works, also titled *The Gleaner*, Murray provides the complete novel.

other periodicals of the age (ibid., 54).[5] Indeed, *The Story of Margaretta* markets itself, in part, as advice and conduct literature. Without further ado, Vigillius succumbs to the requests of his audience and paints a broader portrait of his admirable foster child in *The Story of Margaretta*.

Thus, Murray debunks the negative attitudes about novels, for, after all, her heroine is responsible, intelligent, dedicated to family and friends, reflective, talented, and, most importantly, educated according to the plan of study outlined in Murray's feminist defenses of women's rights and education. While Murray's defense of novelists is a conventional device, it lends a sense of legitimacy to her story and her controversial subject matter. Once she finishes her persuasive argument defending novels and vindicating those who read them, Murray boldly ventures forth into the attempted seduction plot and her theories on women's education.

While visiting friends in New Haven, Connecticut, Margaretta becomes the object of a man's desire—the object of a seducer's gaze. Like many of the seducers and fortune-hunters met in late eighteenth-century American fiction, Sinisterus Courtland is handsome, charismatic, and debonair; however, he is also scheming, persuasive, and manipulative. Courtland becomes particularly captivated by the sixteen-year-old Margaretta after he learns that she comes from a privileged family and may be heir to the Vigillius estate. At this point, Courtland consciously and strategically sets out to seduce Margaretta into marriage in order to gain access to her money. Courtland wishes to return to the wealthy way of life that he had grown accustomed to but lost through poor financial management. Despite his scheming and plotting, Courtland does not anticipate that Margaretta is neither naive nor passive. *The Story of Margaretta* is set apart from other seduction narratives because the

---

5.   Much of the periodical literature of the late eighteenth century was composed of advice to women on their mode of dress, style, behavior, and role in the new republic. For instance, the *Massachusetts Magazine* offered such titles as "Advice to Married Ladies" (June 1793:331–32), "Female Reputation" (July 1793:423–24), "On the Female Accomplishments Most Agreeable to a Husband" (January 1794:37–40), "General Remarks on Women" (January 1794: 20–21), and "On the Conduct of a Young Lady During Courtship" (May 1794:301–2).

heroine does not allow herself to fall prey to a rake. The traditional seduction formula that entails a woman's seduction, abandonment while pregnant, separation from family and friends because of the severe social stigma, and death from consequences of childbirth is interrupted. At this point, the story establishes a link between Margaretta's pained but contemplative decision not to elope with Courtland and her education under her mother's direction.

Within her novel, Murray revises the traditional seduction plot by allowing Margaretta to experience an education that includes subjects traditionally taught only to men. With an education that combines art, sewing, and literature with rhetoric, writing, geography, arithmetic, science, political discussion, astronomy, and bookkeeping, Margaretta, unlike the unfortunate Charlotte Temple and Mary Lumley who did not have the same opportunities, avoids the fatal effects of seduction (ibid., 58–61). In the midst of his description of Margaretta's education under her mother's tutelage, Vigillius deliberately disrupts his narration to address those opponents of female learning who would be dismayed at Margaretta's extensive curriculum: "No, Mr. Pedant, [Margaretta] was not unfitted for her proper sphere; and your stomach, however critical it may be, never digested finer puddings . . . " (ibid., 61). In his witty rebuttal, Vigillius assures his conservative readers that the education of women would not disrupt the domestic sphere or, more specifically, a husband's needs.

In her radical political tract "On the Equality of the Sexes" (1790), Murray contends that learning philosophy, natural sciences, history, and geometry would not take away from a woman's domestic duties such as cookery and clothes making (133–34). Rather, education would enhance her roles as wife and mother. In addition, an intellectually challenging education would encourage young women to reflect, judge, analyze, and critique; these are the skills women need to confront daily life, to make good marriage choices, and to detect profligates. Since seducers encountered in many American seduction narratives often conceal their cunning, manipulative characters behind handsome and charming masks, a young woman needs to be particularly adept at understanding human behavior.

While Murray does illustrate the benefits of female learning, she also represents the fatal consequences experienced by a woman tossed into a hostile world with limited education and no skills to defend herself against villainy. Juxtaposed to Margaretta's story is the tragedy of

Frances Wellwood, who, when left alone in the world after the deaths of her parents, is unable because of lack of education to manage her substantial inheritance properly. Frances falls victim to the artifice of a fortune-hunter. Margaretta learns of Wellwood from her friend, Amelia Worthington, who decides to disclose Frances Wellwood's story to reassure Margaretta of the wisdom of her choice to avoid the notorious seducer, Courtland. In an insightful letter, Amelia Worthington describes to Margaretta the guise a prototypical seducer dons:

> [Courtland's] exterior and deportment . . . are pleasingly fascinating, and our unguarded sex are but too easily captivated. His arts of seduction must be prodigious. When I see you, I will recount the gradual advances, by which he undermined a virtue, that would have been proof against a common assailant. Hoodwinking her reason, and misleading her judgement by arguments the most sophisticated, he induced her to view, as the result of human regulations, the marriage vow. (Murray [1797] 1992, 94)

In order to lead Frances astray, Courtland preys upon the exact qualities society valued in a young woman—silence, passivity, obedience, and naivete. Unskilled in the arts of logic and rhetoric, Frances fails to resist the pressures of her seducer; subsequently, she succumbs to marriage. Once Courtland squanders his wife's inheritance, he abandons her and their children to a life of destitution and dependence upon the charity of friends for survival. Frances must also take to her needle to produce a meager living (ibid., 96). However, Frances has at least this basic skill; Charlotte Temple and Mary Lumley lack not only this skill but the ability to be self-sufficient—to pay rent, to keep house, to earn an income.

Following this account of Frances Wellwood's tragedy, Amelia Worthington encloses another letter for Margaretta, but this one is from the fallen woman herself so she may be given a space to narrate her own story. In her sympathetic letter to Margaretta, Frances reveals her charitable nature toward her seducer. Despite his despicable actions, Courtland, she contends, is not innately corrupt. Frances further argues, "Early indulgence and a mistaken mode of education hath been his ruin" (ibid., 97). Despite Courtland's failings, Frances wants to reclaim him as her husband. Thus Murray allows Frances, who loves her seducer, to remarry him although only because Vigillius pressures Courtland into the reunion.

Although Frances Wellwood's story contains some traditional devices, the novel as a whole integrates these conventional elements with radical ones. On the one hand, Frances Wellwood's reunion with her seducer is a conventional literary device as well as an allusion to Biblical rape laws in which an accused rapist may be allowed to marry his victim. Perhaps this device also explores the question proposed in Richardson's *Clarissa* of whether or not reformed rakes make the best husbands. Nonetheless, this conventional device is problematic, particularly when it is used by a writer who is quite radical and subversive. On the other hand, Murray's novel overtly and covertly challenges puritanical opponents of female learning by illustrating how a well-rounded and guided education can benefit the middle-class woman of the early nation, particularly in the prevention of seduction. Teaching a young woman subjects that engage critical thinking skills—analysis, reflection, inference—can enable her to make the transition from being passive to active. While proper etiquette befitting a privileged woman resonates throughout the novel, certain characteristics—silence, docility, passivity—are not portrayed as befitting a young woman in the active prevention of seduction.

Like the works of Murray and Rowson, Foster's lesser-known fiction, *The Boarding School*, also establishes a link between deficient education and seduction; however, Foster's text illuminates in far greater detail than do *Charlotte Temple* and *The Story of Margaretta* how the study of certain subjects can help a young woman develop the skills necessary to detect rakes and prevent seduction. Foster's *The Boarding School* joined the ongoing debate over female learning by using the seduction narrative to help illustrate instructive lessons on life. Like other novels of the day, *The Boarding School* adopts the convention of being an educational tool, particularly as it is subtitled *Lessons of a Preceptress to Her Pupils Consisting of Information, Instruction, and Advice Calculated to Improve the Manners, and Form the Characters of Young Ladies*. As a work of fiction, *The Boarding School* is divided into three basic sections. The first segment establishes the circumstances behind the founding of the utopic school Harmony Grove. The second section documents a week's curriculum detailing the lectures given by Preceptress Williams and the reasons for her choice of curriculum. The last section is a collection of letters exchanged among the students after they have left Harmony Grove.

The Boarding School puts forth an educational agenda similar to the agenda proposed by Murray in her essays and novel and practiced by Rowson at her Academy. What is particularly interesting about Foster's text is that it provides detailed rationalizations supporting the instructor's choice of subject matter. Like an increasing number of educators of the late eighteenth century, the preceptress of Harmony Grove offers her students a curriculum composed of reading, literature, music, art, religion, geography, and behavioral decorum.

In addition to these staples, the students of Harmony Grove also study history—a subject Benjamin Rush and his colleagues often recommended as a substitute for novel reading. Like her counterparts, Foster defends the incorporation of novel reading into her curriculum when it is used in conjunction with a varied educational program and provides appropriate instruction on manners, behavior, and imaginative creativity. History is studied at Harmony Grove, but not solely from the perspective of chronology or important battles of the world. Rather, history, like literature, provides a medium for reflection and insight regarding the study of human behavior. One student, Cleora Partridge, explains that by observing and studying the conduct of others in history she can detect the deficiencies in their manners and avoid making the same mistakes (Foster 1798, 136). Mrs. Williams explains to her students that history can be used to discern action and motivation, cause and effect, responsibility and consequences:

> Here the various revolutions, the rise, fall, and dismemberment of ancient kingdoms and states may be traced to the different springs of action, in which they originated. Hence you may gain a competent acquaintance with human nature in all its modifications, from the most rude and barbarous, to the most civilized and polished stages of society. (ibid., 25)

In a sense, Mrs. Williams aligns the study of history with the study of psychology and human behavior. This type of investigation provides the necessary prelude to understanding how these skills can help prevent seduction. Foster, though, is not the only writer of her age to include reflections on the importance of women understanding human behavior.

In *Lucy Temple*, Rowson explains that Mary Lumley's imprudent education had made her quick to judge and impetuous ([1828] 1991, 144). Had Mary Lumley possessed, like her friend Lucy Temple, an acute reasoning and knowledge of human behavior, she would not have been hoodwinked by a fortune-hunter (ibid., 182, 241). Because Mary failed to exercise reason in her attachment to Haynes, Lucy warns her to heed the advice of their foster father before choosing to marry. Lucy fears that because Mary is a stranger to the "temper, habits and principles" of Haynes, she will elope with a profligate (ibid., 182). Of course, when she fails to heed the guidance of both Mr. Matthews and Lucy Temple, Mary suffers the fatal effects of being seduced by a fortune-hunter: "deceived, plundered of fortune and good name" (ibid., 225).

On the other hand, Lucy insists that, unlike her friend, she could not be hoodwinked into marriage by a man armed with the rhetoric of romance. The tension created by the juxtaposition of Mary and Lucy emphasizes the need for young women to approach life actively and critically and not to be deceived by "romantic attachments . . . and love at first sight" (ibid., 182). Throughout the story, the narrator emphasizes that Lucy had the benefit of a well-rounded education. As a result, she acts with compassion, acute reasoning, knowledge of human behavior, cultivated taste, and "strong inventive power" (ibid., 241). Although her life is not exempt of tragedy, Lucy is celebrated for teaching, performing charitable works, and founding a school for the education of female children. In the conclusion of the novel, the narrator emphasizes that Lucy contributed significantly to the advancement of women's education. The moral of *Lucy Temple* and *The Boarding School* is that a young woman, if she analyzes human behavior and uses good judgment, can better detect and decipher profligates, seducers, and fortune-hunters from potential friends, acquaintances, and husbands.

In addition to the study of human behavior, *The Boarding School* posits a justification for the teaching of arithmetic and bookkeeping. While Rush argued that arithmetic and bookkeeping were necessary for women to learn so they could help manage the male estate, Foster insisted that, in addition to being able to assist the male estate, women needed to be taught these subjects for their own economic security and independence. Like Murray and Rowson, Foster focused upon the practical applications of history and mathematics. The novels in question established the premise that life is tragic as they debunked the perception that a young woman's marriage automatically secures happiness and financial stability.

At times, women will have to support themselves and their families because of abandonment, the demise of a husband, or the onset of financial difficulty (Foster 1798, 36). Knowledge of bookkeeping would enable women, argued Foster, to earn some income and to manage the household (ibid.). To help illustrate this point, the preceptress of the boarding school shares the story of a young woman named Lucinda who was forced to assume the role of supporter for her family after her father had fallen ill. Because she was encouraged by her father to study arithmetic and bookkeeping, Lucinda was able to assume control over her father's shop and support her family with "ease and reputation" (ibid.). Of course, during the Revolutionary period, it was not unusual for a wife or daughter to manage the farm, business, and household while the men of the family were occupied with battle.

Foster and Murray also argued that for its ability to assist cognitive skill development, the practice of writing should be an essential component of the curriculum. At Harmony Grove, composition can be both entertaining and instructive in inducing reflection. Like Margaretta's parents, Mrs. Williams maintains that the writing and revising of thoughts and reflections can help students polish their expressions, improve their opinions, and better formulate their logic and reason—three important tenets of Enlightenment philosophy that are taught in conjunction with the arts, creative writing, and literature (ibid., 31).

Harmony Grove, Mrs. Williams implies, is a place where young women can develop and express their talents with support and encouragement rather than ridicule and condemnation. Mrs. Williams embraces republican rhetoric and incorporates republican ideology into her governing philosophy when she proclaims that American women are very fortunate to live in a land that fosters rather than suppresses their intellectual pursuits: "Thrice blessed are we, the happy daughters of this land of liberty, where the female mind is unshackled by the restraints of tyrannical custom, which in many other regions confines the exertions of genius to the usurped powers of lordly man!" (ibid.). Perhaps Mrs. Williams alludes to a time when colonial America curtailed women from fully developing their talents and desires for intellectual growth. Of course, Mrs. Williams engages her students, as Foster engages her readers, with a bit of hyperbole. Mrs. Williams of Harmony Grove certainly encourages women's intellectual and creative development, but she is also being overzealous in her optimism for female learning. Foster knew all too well the controversial debate over female education, but at the utopic Harmony Grove, gender boundaries are broken down. During the postrevolutionary age, women were in fact still struggling to free themselves from the shackles that bound their bodies, minds, and spirits, which ultimately prevented them from tasting the fruits of liberty.

Perhaps at this point in *The Boarding School* Mrs. Williams answers the rhetorical question posed by Murray in "On the Equality of the Sexes." Like Foster, Murray believed that women are creative, intellectual beings with powerful minds and imaginations. In her radical feminist tract arguing for the natural equality of men and women, Murray raises a question about the validity of the circumscribed lot that traditionally discouraged women from developing creatively and intellectually: "Is the needle and kitchen sufficient to employ the operations of a soul thus organized?" (1790, 133). From the perspective of Mrs. Williams, the answer is no.

Most certainly, Murray and Foster were not the only women to defend a woman's right to intellectual development or to ponder the question of whether or not a woman's hand was fit for only a needle. This question was pondered one hundred forty years earlier by Anne Bradstreet, a colonial American, in her poem "The Prologue":

I am obnoxious to each carping tongue
Who says my hand a needle better fits,
A poet's pen all scorn I should thus wrong.
For such despite they cast on female wits:
If what I do prove well, it won't advance,
They'll say it's stol'n, or else it was by chance. ([1650] 1994, 200)

Like her descendants, Bradstreet reflects not only upon the traditional hostility a woman had to contend with if she were learned, but also the excuses often given to account for a woman's intelligence or ability to create such works as poetry and essays.[6] Both Murray and Foster offer a defense of female improvement, particularly creative development. A woman, implies Foster and argues Murray in "On the Equality of the Sexes," can reason only from what she knows (1790, 133). If a girl or young woman is denied intellectual development, then she is forced to remain in a state of perpetual childhood. While both Murray and Foster critiqued Enlightenment philosophy for its noted misogyny, they also called for certain aspects of Enlightenment thought to be extended to women. Contrary to the stances taken by Locke and Rousseau, Murray, Foster, and Rowson believed women to be intellectual, rational beings, capable of evolving into a mature consciousness.

To help young women cultivate their talents and intellect, Mrs. Williams includes with each daily lesson a story or narrative to illustrate the importance of studying a variety of subjects in balance. The tragedy of Levitia is one of many formula narratives employed at Harmony Grove to impart vital information about the complexities of life and the importance of reflection in the making of pivotal decisions that can determine the course of a young woman's adult life. Levitia, like her counterparts in other stories, falls victim to the artifice of a fortune-hunter. Mrs. Williams links Levitia's inability to resist flattery and declarations of love from a "deluding libertine" to a misinformed education. Because she lacks critical-thinking skills, Levitia hastily elopes with a man who promises her wealth and fortune. This one act plummets Levitia into a state of poverty and despair (Foster 1798, 42–43). Had Levitia the benefit of a

---

6. Ironically, in the preface to her "On the Equality of the Sexes," Murray contends that her work was not plagiarized, just as Bradstreet insisted that her work was not plagiarized. In "The Gleaner Unmasked," Murray notes that Rousseau insisted that women who do write are dependent upon men for guidance. Murray assures her readers that no man guided the creation of her works (1797, 805).

In the preface to its 1790 publication, Murray claimed that "On the Equality of the Sexes" was actually published eleven years earlier in 1779. This essay predates Mary Wollstonecraft's *A Vindication of the Rights of Woman*.

more balanced education, she would have been able to reflect upon her marriage choice, examine the consequences of quick, irrational decision-making, and ultimately avoid the fatal effects of seduction. Mrs. Williams insists that she has synthesized an educational program that will teach students to think and act for themselves (ibid., 48). Maria Williams, the daughter of the preceptress, shares with a former student her appreciation of honest and frank stories about young women who have fallen prey to treachery and deceit because they are lessons that can be incorporated into the classroom since they warn by example and inform by discussion (ibid., 193).

The inclusion of seduction narratives also helps Mrs. Williams to counsel her students on personal development. Like the parents of Margaretta in *The Story of Margaretta*, Mrs. Williams encourages reflection on one's daily activities and one's place in the world (ibid., 49). The ancient Greek adage "know thyself" provides the foundation for this reflection. In other words, Mrs. Williams encourages her students to develop their self-awareness. This is not a belief or recommendation particular to Foster and Murray. Rowson also explores the importance of self-knowledge in *Lucy Temple*. In one scene, a mother relates the story of her fallen daughter, Alice Lonsdale, rather ironically to the soon-to-be seduced Mary Lumley and her guardian, Matthews. Alice's mother notes that she encouraged her daughter to develop only her artistic talents rather than her intellectual ones. More importantly, Alice's mother admits that she "did not teach her [daughter] to know herself" (Rowson [1828] 1991, 157). As a result, Alice was hastily married and consequently overburdened with debts after her husband's incarceration. Self-understanding and a balanced education, argue Murray, Rowson, and Foster, encourage self-mastery, the control of one's mind, body, and spirit. The practice of introspection, proposes Mrs. Williams, will allow young women to understand their "passions, affections, and propensities" (Foster 1798, 49). Self-understanding coupled with an education that engages critical thinking can prepare young women to cope with a fundamentally hostile and tragic world; this underlying premise resonates throughout the novels under review.

A young woman, Mrs. Williams further argues, unskilled in the ways of the world "is very apt to be misled by the adulation which is offered at the shrine of vanity. She is considered as a mark for the wit of every coxcomb, who wishes to display his gallantry" (ibid., 50). Mrs. Williams assumes that the average young middle-class woman is easily led astray by vanity and flattery. Skilled in debauchery and persuasion, the artful seducer can entice a young woman away from the use of reason and judgment. However, if a young woman practices reflection and demonstrates self-knowledge of her merits and accomplishments as does the student Julia Greenfield, she can detect the hyperbole and cunning tactics of adversaries (ibid.).

Ultimately, education at Harmony Grove seeks to prepare the women of the new nation to meet life's challenges, including the challenges presented by rakes and profligates. By elevating the status of women and stressing their importance to the nation, Harmony Grove debunks the common myths about learned women shared by many American opponents of female learning. In a letter to a friend, Matilda Fielding, a student at Harmony Grove, reflects upon the perceptions of women as vain and imprudent and concludes: "I trust that our improved country women are rising far superior to [these myths], and are able to convince the world, that the American fair are enlightened, generous, and liberal" (ibid., 151). Matilda Fielding's letter reveals some interesting insights about the status of women in her culture. Women are not only aware of the negative images constructing their lives, but they also no longer want to be subjected to them. Thus, women choose to participate actively in the transformation of the myths that govern their lives.

On a fundamental level, the novelists in question aligned learning with consciousness raising. Significant changes in education and the prevention of seduction could come about only when society transformed its views of women and women transformed their views of themselves. For these authors, the basis of this transformation was linked with a woman's understanding of self and society. In essence, the underlying philosophy that appeared to guide the novelists under consideration was a transformational one. Today, many theorists of women's issues, including Teresa Ebert, often view feminism as a transformational theory and practice that seeks to advance the lives of women. In "The Difference of Postmodern Feminism," Ebert notes that feminism is "a cultural critique and practice of social change that seeks to transform" power relations between men and women (1991, 888). Murray, Rowson, Foster, and Tenney certainly demonstrated this sensibility when they called for the transformation of educational systems and the elimination of seduction. These authors led a fervent call for women to participate actively in the transformational process by shifting their own views of certain customs and the traditional means of social organization. From a Jungian perspective, an individual consciousness is part of a mass consciousness. When a small number of people move into a new level of understanding, this change in consciousness or perspective may indeed influence the consciousness of others. While the consciousness raising encouraged by Murray, Rowson, and Foster may have influenced only a small segment of the population or the masses—the young females of the middle- and upper-classes—it still may have provided the necessary impetus for additional change. Change may occur first at an individual level and then eventually on a societal one.

Dorcasina Sheldon embraces this transformational philosophy in Tenney's *Female Quixotism*, but she is ironically viewed by her family and friends as a woman suffering from a mistaken education and novel-mania, or excessive novel reading. Similar to other novels of the age, *Female Quixotism* is cast as a didactic text—one that will teach the reader to "Learn to be wise by others harm" (Tenney [1801] 1992, 4). In particular, *Female Quixotism* is addressed to the young women of the new republic who read novels and romances. Within the letter that prefaces the novel, the narrator claims that the biography of Dorcasina will teach young women to avoid disaster and disgrace brought about by the unrestrained perusal of novels (ibid., 3). In "The Parodic Mode," Cynthia Miecznikowksi argues that Tenney's novel is a satire of the misinformed criticism of the novel (1990, 35). But it is also, as Cathy Davidson proposes in *Revolution and The Word*, a satire of a society with a deficient educational system and limited roles for women (1986, 187).

As a privileged Pennsylvanian woman and heir to a substantial fortune, Dorcasina had the benefit of private instructors and an extensive family library (Tenney [1801] 1992, 5). While the subjects of Dorcasina's lessons are not detailed, the narrator emphasizes that Dorcasina "made great proficiency" in all of them (ibid.). The narrator, like the narrator of *The Story of Margaretta*, also provides a defense of Dorcasina's learning by fervently condemning the "enemies of female education" who "thought a woman had no business with any book but the Bible, or perhaps the art of cookery; believing that every thing beyond these served only to disqualify her for the duties of domestic life" (ibid., 14). On another level, *Female Quixotism* presents some rather startling representations of both learned women and men. Many of Dorcasina's thoughts, actions, and desires are ascribed as misadventures, fantasies, and irrational life choices. While Tenney does include Dorcasina in scenes that parody the works of Richardson, Fielding, and a variety of other European authors, she also includes Dorcasina in scenes that depict her as an astute, intelligent, reflective, considerate, and charitable individual.

More importantly, Dorcasina is presented as a woman with great aspirations who, because of her gender, has no legitimate channel for these aspirations to manifest themselves. Despite its dismissal by the narrator as a flight of fancy, Dorcasina's view on the abolition of slavery attests to her thoughtful and perceptive character. In one scene, Dorcasina and her servant Betty reflect upon the kind of life Dorcasina would have if she were the wife of her suitor, the slave-owner Lysander, for Dorcasina believes that she would be quite influential in liberating Lysander's slaves. The narrator describes Dorcasina's reflections upon this act by relating:

> [Dorcasina] then indulged herself in the agreeable, humane, but romantic idea, that, being the wife of Lysander, she could become the benefactress of his slaves. She even extended her benevolent reveries beyond the plantation of her future husband, and, wrapt in the glow of enthusiasm, saw his neighbors imitating his example, and others imitating them, till the spirit of justice and humanity should extend to the utmost limits of the United States, and all the blacks be emancipated from bondage. (ibid., 9)

Dorcasina appears to embrace the kind of transformational agenda embraced by Murray, Rowson, and Foster; that is, Dorcasina embraces the theory that a transformation of mass consciousness begins with a transformation of individual consciousness. Although her reflections are dismissed as romantic indulgences and "pleasing illusions," Dorcasina's views on the abolition of slavery foreshadow not only women's progression from theorists to activists in the nineteenth century but also the coming of Sarah and Angelina Grimké, pioneering abolitionists and activists for women's rights.

Although Dorcasina reveals a sensitivity to the psychological ramifications of slavery upon the enslaved, there are problems with her views of slavery and transformation. In their introduction to *Female Quixotism*, Jean Nienkamp and Andrea Collins note that the novel offers rich examples of the class structure of the early nation (1992, xix). Indeed, Dorcasina's discussion of slavery certainly offers a rich illustration of both class and gender issues. In particular, Dorcasina realizes that her role in the emancipation of slaves can only be accomplished as the wife of Lysander, and that as the wife of a plantation owner and a member of the privileged class she can exert her authority over African Americans by hiring them as servants. On some level, Dorcasina understands that there are boundaries placed upon her gender just as she understands that her class has privileged her over others. Despite the novel's insistence that Dorcasina misreads novels and perhaps at times is unable to distinguish reality from fantasy, she is represented as quick, astute, and intelligent in her reflections on slavery and politics. Whatever her education might have included in addition to novel reading, Dorcasina is certainly not deceptive, belligerent, or unscrupulous, as are the men who try to seduce her.

Armed with the rhetoric of romance, the seducers and fortune-hunters who traverse the pages of *Female Quixotism* continually commit the most violent and deceptive atrocities against women. For instance, when a young man native to Connecticut is first introduced in *Female Quixotism*, he is described as "an excellent scholar, a genius and a wag" (Tenney [1801] 1992, 104). Ironically, Philander, a graduate of New Haven College (now Yale), appropriates the language of novels and romances to deceive, then lure Dorcasina into physically and verbally abusive situations in which he is the primary perpetrator. In a particular scene, Philander's cross-dressing provides the necessary guise for him to physically batter Dorcasina and Betty by pulling their hair and tearing their clothes (ibid., 115). Throughout this account, the narrator notes that Philander is a "mischief loving scholar" (ibid., 116). When Philander is first introduced into the story, the narrator comments that, although the scholar had played numerous pranks and tricks on other individuals, he was not vicious (ibid., 104). While he may not have been malicious to his tutors, Philander certainly demonstrates this brutality towards women. Of course, the dissonance between the characterization of Philander as a mischievous adventurer and his actual abusive treatment of women reveals how often violence against women is misinterpreted or met with indifference. By including detailed accounts of the abuse of women, *Female Quixotism* reveals a reality that is often concealed.

The novels of Murray, Rowson, Tenney, and Foster certainly address social issues—marriage, seduction, violence—that many middle-class female readers grappled with in their daily lives. However, these novels also demonstrate that a revising of traditional education is essential for better preparing women to deal with the complexity of life. More particularly, an education that engages critical thinking can help women actively to prevent seduction. In their essays and textbooks, both Murray and Rowson recognize that education and socialization go hand in hand. If traditional educational programs are going to change, then so must traditional socialization practices. In *The Bonds of Womanhood*, Nancy Cott explains that the controversy over women's education and their new roles in the early nation encouraged women "to understand gender as the essential determinant of their lives" (1977, 123).

Most certainly, Murray, like her friends Abigail Adams and Mercy Warren, understood that gender determined not only the amount of education girls and young women would receive during the eighteenth century but also differences in childrearing customs. In "On the Equality of the Sexes," Murray challenges opponents of female improvement when she questions: "Will it be said that the judgment of a male of two years old, is more sage than that of a female's of the same age? I believe the reverse is generally observed to be true" (1790, 133). With the minds of males and females equal in their ability to learn, Murray identified the source of the disparity between the education of girls and boys not in nature but in socialization.

Murray's contemporary, Rowson, expresses similar sentiments in *A Present for Young Ladies* (1811) bestowed upon her students at graduation. In this collection of works by Rowson and her students, Rowson begins to question the sources that keep women in powerless positions: "[Women] are generally called the weaker sex and perhaps through constitution, habit, and education in some degree they are so: but there have been numberless instances of women who have proved themselves adequate to every trial . . . " (1811, 90). Both Rowson in her *Exercises in History* (1822) and Murray in her "Observations on Female Abilities" (1798) list many notable women, such as Queen Elizabeth I, Mary Wollstonecraft, and Mercy Otis Warren, who made valuable contributions to their culture. Neither Murray nor Rowson would have agreed with traditionalists who expressed the views of Rousseau or Chesterfield in "On the Happy Influence Arising From Female Society" from the *Massachusetts Magazine* (July 1785) and argued that women were essentially weak, timid, defenseless, and in need of men for protection (220–23).

Murray and Rowson believed that traditional views of women and socialization prevented women from fully reaping the fruits of education. In "On the Equality of the Sexes," Murray observes that boys are often encouraged to anticipate formal education and civic duties while girls are taught to be "domesticated, . . . confined and limited" (1790, 133). The traditional socialization of girls has consequences, contends Murray. When a female arrives at womanhood, she comes to a startling recognition:

> [She] feels a void, which the employments allotted her are by no means capable of filling. . . . Meantime she herself is most unhappy; she feels the want of a cultivated mind. . . . She experiences a mortifying consciousness of inferiority, which embitters every enjoyment. (ibid., 133)

Perhaps the void experienced by many women is akin to the devaluation experienced by all those individuals in society who are relegated to the margins as the Other. In *The Coloniser and the Colonised*, Albert Memmi explains that the Other is perceived to lack the qualities and options valued by colonialists or neocolonialists (1965, 83). Indeed, Murray contends that women arrive at a point in their adult lives where they realize that many of the differences between men and women are socially constructed, and that women in general are perceived to lack many valued characteristics—wisdom, intelligence, rationalism— because of their gender. This recognition or consciousness of the dissonance between men and women, at least of the same race and class, leaves women, according to Murray, feeling unfulfilled and disappointed.

Murray's sensitivity to the psychological ramifications of restriction, limitation, and devaluation pervades her writings. In fact, Murray's insights and concerns are in some instances quite existential for a woman who experienced both the Enlightenment and the Romantic age. While she places a significant value upon women's roles as wives and mothers, Murray also emphasizes that women need more to their lives than cookery and housekeeping. In "Observations on Female Abilities," Murray insists that women should be encouraged to develop their talents, intellect and interests. In Foster's *The Coquette*, Mrs. Richman reveals to her friend Eliza Wharton that her sole happiness rests in the domains of domesticity; however, Foster points out, as do Rowson and Tenney, that the domains of domesticity are not exempt of tragedy. Murray certainly does not suggest that women eliminate the realm of domesticity or relinquish their roles as wives and mothers, for Murray herself embraced both roles as she evolved them. However, Murray does suggest that women need more to their existence than their service to others: Women should fulfill their desire for intellectual and creative development.

In her essay "Sentiments of Education" (1797), Murray explores a mother's central role in early childhood development, particularly her role in guiding the development of her children's psyches, talents, and abilities. "Sentiments of Education" contends that a mother can exert a crucial amount of influence over both her son and daughter, and if she is going to embrace her role as nurturer and guide, she too must be encouraged to be educated. Mothers need to be educated not only in art and literature but also in history and natural sciences. While children are growing up, mothers could use their resources and teach children a variety of lessons. With an orange, a mother could create a globe as a visual aid for a geography lesson. From a fire, a mother could instruct upon the elements of light and heat, the seasons, and the solar system. Indeed, mothers are essential to the fostering of children's intellectual growth and moral development, for mothers imprint on formidable young minds ideas, character, and morality (Murray 1797, 287).

Ultimately, the changed role for mothers that Murray, Rowson, and Foster formulated in their essays and novels was the role Linda Kerber has dubbed republican motherhood: the belief or ideology that women were being called to assume a more pivotal role in the early nation than they had ever before been called to perform. In *Women of the Republic*, Kerber explains that mothers were expected to dedicate their lives, albeit indirectly, to civic service; mothers were rearing sons who would be future citizens, politicians, and lawyers—those who would steer the young nation into the future (1980, 228–29). While occupying this newly recognized role, a mother also needed to be the perfect wife by maintaining the realm of domesticity so that her husband could pursue the political world where he could be, according to the Enlightenment philosophy of Rousseau and Locke that was embraced by the nation's founding fathers, the intelligent, rational being he was meant to be. According to Cott, mothers were expected to "generate and regenerate" the nation's moral character and future (1977, 97). During this period, the role of mother certainly began to be acknowledged publicly and cherished for its instrumental contributions. Indeed, illustrations of the importance of the ideal republican mother and teacher are found in the novels under review. However, the role of republican mother defined women in strictly utilitarian terms and in relationship to men. Despite the problems inherent in the ideology of republican motherhood, Kerber explains that this perspective on the new roles of mothers certainly encouraged females to be educated beyond basic literacy—perhaps the first steps in the revising of women's education (ibid., 200).

For Murray, Rowson, and Foster, the role of republican mother needed to be extended from the home to the classroom. In "Sentiments on Education," Murray explains that the preceptor, like the parent, should be sensible, patient, benevolent, honest, sensitive, and contrary to inflicting harsh punishment—everything perhaps that La Rue was not to her student Charlotte of *Charlotte Temple* ([1791] 1986, 288–89). If La Rue had been more sensitive to the concerns of a young woman, she would have neither persuaded Charlotte into having clandestine meetings with Montraville nor later rejected her when she was abandoned by Montraville. The kind of instructor Murray calls for stands in sharp contrast to both La Rue and the traditional Puritan perception that permeated New England schooling traditions of an instructor as harsh disciplinarian. According to Lyle Koehler in *A Search for Power*, Puritans believed that children were susceptible to sinful impulses. In order to prevent the manifestation of sinful behavior, strict discipline by adults and obedience by children in education and childrearing were essential. Koehler

further concludes that children both within the home and at school were kept in a state of "repressive bondage," and the rod was particularly favored as a punitive device to help re-enforce the importance of control and discipline (1980, 13). Murray calls for the direct reversal of this Puritan philosophy of teaching. In "Sentiments on Education," she establishes her position on early childhood education very clearly when she asks austere instructors to "spare the rod" and ultimately their severe style of teaching for more nurturing, reward-orientated techniques that would encourage learning (Murray [1797] 1992, 291). Murray's "Sentiments on Education" is particularly groundbreaking for the age because she explores the psychology behind teaching and learning (ibid., 289).

While Murray theorized about teaching styles in her essays and explored the long-term benefits of the education of both mothers and daughters in *The Story of Margaretta*, Rowson was actually busy practicing her nurturing educational style as the founder and preceptress of a female academy in Massachusetts. Proof of Rowson's devotion to fostering the development of young women is found among the letters of her students. The fourteen-year-old Eliza Southgate writes to her sister who was a student at Rowson's school "that no woman was ever better calculated to govern a school than Mrs. Rowson. She governs by the love with which she always inspires her scholars" (Woody 1966, 58). Rowson was indeed the apotheosis of the republican mother figure in education.

For a variety of other reasons, Rowson was an innovator in women's education during the late eighteenth and early nineteenth centuries. In addition to being a dramatist, songwriter, poet, essayist, and novelist, the English-born Rowson was an educator in her adopted home, Massachusetts. According to her biographer Elias Nason, Rowson's role as preceptress and founder of the Young Ladies Academy (1797) won her a considerable amount of respect and recognition in her community. Rowson's academy was in such demand that she could not accommodate all the prospective applicants in her school that held approximately one hundred students (Nason 1870, 90). In particular, Nason notes that Rowson had a special quality as a teacher:

Loving ardently the pursuit of literature, she had the rare and happy faculty, without which no instructor can succeed, of inspiring others with her own emotions. Her enthusiasm awoke enthusiasms. She was moreover, systematic, dignified, persist-ent. Her school became the topic of conversation in the fashion-able circles, and applications for admission to it were made from every section of the country. (ibid., 100)

Of course, Eliza Southgate's letters to her sister attest to Rowson's unique ability to inspire learning. Unwavering in her devotion to her stu-dents, Rowson transferred her skills as a novelist dedicated to the edu-cation of the American fair to textbook writing. Her authorship of six textbooks ranging from spelling and reading to geography and history attests to her desire to prevent young women from experiencing a "mis-taken education" and its potential consequences explored in her narra-tives of seduction.

Dissatisfied with the traditional textbooks available to students, Rowson created her own history books. But instead of providing her stu-dents, who came from as far as the West Indies, merely with accounts of male accomplishments, Rowson included reports about distinguished women. In particular, Rowson's *Exercises in History* (1822) demon-strates her desire to make learning creative when she employs the ques-tion and answer format to relay historical and biographical information. During a lesson on Roman history, a student may have pondered:

Q. What illustrious female lived about A.D. 1081?
A. Anna Commina, daughter to the emperor Alexius Commenus, whose elegant writings gave celebrity to her father's reign. About this time the Turks invaded the eastern empire, and they finally conquered Asia minor, A.D. 1084. (Rowson 1822, 56)

Rowson's history book, in particular, exemplifies her choice to allow her female students to read about female accomplishments and the impor-tance of women in history. According to Memmi, the colonized often cease to be a subject of history (1965, 92), but Rowson reinstates women's place in historical development and emphasizes their valuable contributions.

History, though, was not the only subject students were studying at Rowson's academy. Reading, writing, arithmetic, literature, geography, spelling, drawing, painting, embroidery, geometry, science, and piano—the same varied subject matter proposed by Murray and Foster—provided the staples of the curriculum (Nason 1870, 104). Like Mrs. Williams of the fictitious Harmony Grove, Rowson also educated her students on behavioral decorum and provided wise counsel whenever they needed comforting (ibid.). Although Rowson's academy was quite unlike most female academies of the late eighteenth century, it was particularly revolutionary in that it included and encouraged public speaking, despite Biblical and Puritan prohibitions (Weil 1976, 79). Opponents of women's public speaking often used St. Paul's injunctions against women speaking in church, teaching, and using authority over men to reprimand vocal women (I Timothy 2:11–12). Despite these religious injunctions and the stigmas attached to women who violated them, Rowson provided special forums and recitals for her students to engage in public speaking with dignity. Most certainly, Rowson's groundbreaking advocacy of women's public speaking predates notable nineteenth-century revolutionaries of public speaking: Frances Wright, a lecturer advocating women's education and rights; the Grimké sisters, abolitionists from South Carolina; Elizabeth Cady Stanton and Susan B. Anthony, pioneers in the women's rights movement.

Like Murray and Foster, Rowson vehemently defended a woman's right to education despite opponents who equated female learning with masculine pursuits and the disruption of gender roles. In *A Present for Young Ladies*, Rowson assures her Mr. Pedants, just as Bradstreet, Murray, and Tenney assured their Mr. Pedants:

> There is no reason why we should stop short in the career of knowledge; though it has been asserted by the other sex that the distaff, the needle, together with domestic concerns alone should occupy the time of women. . . . when literature, or the study of the fine arts, can be engaged in, without the neglect of our feminine duties, why may not we attain the goal of perfection as well as the other sex. (1811, 84–85)

Rowson went to great lengths to defend the teaching of her most beloved subjects—art, music, and literature—to her students. But even she realized that the education of women needed to be composed of a variety of subjects to better prepare young women for their future of "feminine duties"—wife, mother, household manager. Like Murray, Foster, and Tenney, Rowson was not calling for the eradication of women's roles as wives and mothers but for a transformation of them.

Perhaps Murray had Rowson in mind when she congratulated women in her "Observations on Female Abilities" (1798) for their instrumental role in "the happy revolution" of women's education (702–3). The rise of female academies, Murray contended, would play a vital role in paving the way for educational reform. Murray recognized that transforming the power relations between men and women, particularly in education, was a time-consuming process of both revolution and evolution. The rise of female academies, argued Murray, would spark a new direction in women's history.

The philosophies of Murray, Rowson, Tenney, and Foster were both revolutionary and evolutionary. These authors clearly discovered that the traditional way of organizing society and viewing women's place in the social hierarchy provided neither a productive nor a fulfilling way of life for those marginalized individuals most susceptible to seduction. Most certainly, these authors called not for an eradication of the systems that constructed their lives but rather for a transformation of them, beginning with education. This transformation of women's education would help transform women from passive victims to active preventers of seduction.

By voicing their views through their novels, essays, and textbooks, these four novelists challenged the dominant logic—dislodging to some extent its hegemony—and exposed the misogyny and egocentrism that informed traditional education curricula for women. By proposing both alternative ways of viewing educated women and alternative educational programs, these four authors not only sparked the formation of a new history for women in a new nation, but they also sparked the process of decolonization.

Part of this process of decolonization involves empowering young women with the necessary knowledge and confidence to repossess their minds, bodies, and spirits—their lives. Nancy Hartsock argues that decolonization struggles often "represent the diverse and disorderly Others beginning to demand to be heard and beginning to chip away at the social and political power of the theorizer" (1990, 163). Hartsock

also notes that decolonization has two basic features—critique and construction (ibid.). Both features pervade the works of Murray, Rowson,
Foster, and Tenney, for these authors do not offer a critique of traditional
educational curricula and seduction without proposing solutions. Once
young women are armed with the necessary education to take back their
lives, they can participate actively in the prevention of seduction.

2
Declarations of Independence: Seduction and the Disenfranchised Woman

"THE DYE IS CAST," sadly concludes Mr. Matthews of *Lucy Temple* immediately after he learns that his ward, Mary Lumley, has been seduced into marriage by a fortune-hunter (Rowson [1828] 1991, 190). Variations of Julius Caesar's ominous words of impending doom resonate most appropriately throughout the seduction narratives of Rowson and Foster because they relate the inevitable journey of tragedy a heroine embarks upon once she has been seduced. The conventional seduction paradigm of the American eighteenth-century novel—seduction, pregnancy, abandonment—can also be expanded to include the inherent legal crisis a young middle- or upper-class woman might face when she boldly declares her independence from patriarchal authority.

In addition to enlightening the American fair about the correlation between seduction and pregnancy and about the need for women to experience an education that engages critical thinking, the seduction novels of Rowson, Foster, Tenney, and Murray warn young women about the dangers that might await them if they declare their independence prematurely. More specifically, the seduction narratives warn young women about the failure of America's Declaration of Independence to include them. Quite often critics fail to consider the novels under review as cultural critiques that expose what is at stake for a particular group of women in the new nation if patriarchal and neocolonialist perspectives on power and gender relations, the constricted roles of women, and the laws that keep women in subservient, dependent positions are not transformed.

Indeed, the American Revolution was not completely revolutionary in the alteration of the traditional relationships between men and women of different races and classes. In her examination of the postrevolutionary status of women, Marylynn Salmon provides some interesting reflections upon what the legal rights of women often reveal about a culture. Salmon notes that a woman's economic independence in a society indicates her position in that society. For instance, a society that supports independent women supports their complete authority over their property. On the other hand, a society that "prefers passive or subservient women places their property in the hands of others—fathers or husbands" (Salmon 1979, 86).

A principal way of securing the middle-class woman's traditional status as the weaker sex or the colonized Other in the new nation was to legally force her to surrender her property and inheritances to her husband upon marriage. Although the patriots fought to free themselves from their mother country and everything that linked them with England, they, in turn, became neocolonialists by conveniently maintaining certain English laws to help secure their privileged status over women and men of other races and classes. According to English common law absorbed into the legal system of the early nation, a married woman's legal rights were "covered" by her husband. The *Feme Covert* or "hidden woman" and the law of coverture assumed that a husband and a wife upon marriage merged into one unit; however, many scholars recognize that this one unit referred only to the husband (Hymowitz and Weissman 1978, 22). In a sense, a woman's colonized status was further secured upon marriage when she figuratively suffered a civil death. In particular, the narratives in question reveal a striking concern over the property rights a woman had to relinquish when she became a wife. Unless a prenuptial agreement was formulated, a woman was legally expected to relinquish her inheritance and any other personal property to her husband upon marriage (Benson 1935, 235). To further secure her legal death and colonized status, the married woman or the *Feme Covert* could not vote, collect her own wages, attend college, sign contracts, sue in a court of law, or in some states possess legal rights over her own children for the children were the property of the father. If a wife was legally defined as property and was theoretically akin to the status of chattel, then she had no rights as a citizen nor a voice recognized by the law (Fisher 1975, 40).

On the other hand, the single, white woman or widow over the age of eighteen or the *Feme Sole* did have the right to own property and collect her own wages. However, like the married woman, she still had neither voice nor representation in a government that demanded she pay taxes and abide by the laws (Hymowitz and Weissman 1978, 22). The single privileged woman certainly did not enjoy all the rights of the property owner, but women of other races and classes had even fewer rights, if any at all. If a woman was relegated to the domestic realm, she, like the colonized Other, could not enter the public or political realm. With no access to university education, a woman certainly could not enter the professional workplace. Because a woman was not part of official culture, her rights and concerns were met with indifference.

Despite the new nation's calculated disregard of women's concerns and rights, the American Revolution, observes Mary Beth Norton in *Liberty's Daughters*, did have a crucial effect upon the lives of eighteenth-century women; but this impact was not overtly evidenced in the political realm. Rather, the private writings of women attest to their discontent with their limited roles and rights during the early national period (Norton 1980, xv). In addition to women's private writings, women's sentimental literature provides evidence of the Revolution's impact upon the thinking of New England women and their desire to forewarn republican daughters approaching the most pivotal decision of their lives about the inherent dangers of their political disenfranchisement.

The seduction narratives of Murray, Foster, Tenney, and Rowson illuminate women's political disenfranchisement during the early national period by drawing a link between seduction and the American Revolution's failure to extend unalienable rights to women. The revolutionary fervor of America's transition from dependence to independence pervaded the lives of many middle- and upper-class women. The novels under evaluation illuminate not only young women's dissatisfaction with their traditional lots, but also the problems young women would face when they declared their independence in a political environment unwilling to support women's appropriation of unalienable rights. Young readers needed to understand that their lives subsequent to their declarations of independence had the potential of ending in seduction, abandonment, and poverty if they were not well prepared to meet their new lot. Of all the narratives in question, *Lucy Temple* most overtly challenges the patriarchy's concept of the *Feme Covert* by representing the tragic legal hardship women must endure when they prematurely declare their independence from patriarchal authority.

Although the sequel to *Charlotte Temple* takes place in England, it still reflects the American woman's discontent with patriarchal authority and her prescribed lot. What is particularly interesting about Mary Lumley's situation is that, despite warnings against forming a union with a fortune-hunter, she chooses to marry Stephen Haynes because she ardently desires to exercise her rights as a *Feme Sole*; that is, Mary desires to exercise as much authority over herself as possible (Rowson [1828] 1991, 181). She wants to make her own choices about the direction of her future. In her anthropological exploration of the genesis of women's oppression, Gayle Rubin observes that in a society that exchanges women for economic and political reasons, a woman lacks all rights to herself (1975, 177). This is the crux of Mary's crisis. As significant a step as this longing for independence is for a woman who wants to be self-determining, the social environment in which she lives is reluctant to grant her this right. Because the eighteenth-century woman dwells in an environment that legally prefers passive and subservient women, she has very few legal rights. When a woman asserts her self-appointed right to leave her paternal base and enter into a relationship with a man of her choice rather than the choice of a patriarchal figure, she is perceived as a deviant who challenges patriarchal authority and disrupts the social order (ibid.).

Indeed, Mary's desire to escape her home erupts into a conflict with Matthews, her guardian. After he learns of her attachment to a profligate, Matthews insists that Mary consult with him before making any decision to marry. Her desire to marry, though, appears to be spurred more by a power struggle with Matthews than a love for Haynes. To a large extent, Mary longs for her coming of age and the law's recognition of her ability "to dispose" of her own person. In her bold declaration of independence, Mary exclaims: " . . . in a short period the law will consider me of age to dispose of my own person, and take care of my own interest" (Rowson [1828] 1991, 181). Although she loves the Matthews family, Mary is so dedicated to her concept of independence that she admits that she "cannot solicit permission to do what I like, and go where I please, from persons who . . . have no right now to control me" (ibid., 187). Clearly, Mary wants to exert control over her life; she wants to repossess herself from the control of her father figure.

The narratives of seduction by Murray, Foster, Rowson, and Tenney all mark the stage just before a young woman's marriage as a pivotal transition period. In a sense, this stage of transition reflects the transition period of America. Although America is no longer connected with her parent country, she is still quite inexperienced in the particulars of democratic theory. As the Jungian psychologist Clarissa Estes notes, stories often relate information that can benefit an individual's psychic development because they impart vital information that will help a reader or listener move on to the next stage of her life (1992, 15). In both *Charlotte Temple* and *Lucy Temple*, Rowson uses her dramatic flair for storytelling to help guide young women and perhaps even the young nation into the next phase of their lives.

Most appropriately, Rowson gives her female readers essential information concerning their status once they reach adulthood and declare their independence. When young women reach adulthood, they need to exercise intelligence and good judgment. Rowson's portrayal of Mary attests to the tragedy that can befall a woman when she makes hasty decisions. Once she becomes an adult as defined by the law, Mary declares her independence, but this declaration circumvents intensive thought and preparation. She fails to heed the advice of friends and family who are concerned about her well-being. While he represents the patriarchal presence throughout the novel, Matthews wants to prevent his wards from marrying profligates, particularly when most of the young women have some form of inheritance, and, thus, proper "settlements need to be made" (Rowson [1828] 1991, 181). Rowson's novels emphasize that a woman can rightfully declare her independence only after she receives the necessary education and guidance to prepare for this new lot. While Mary wants to control her life, she fails to understand that she needs to protect herself legally from rakes and fortune-hunters. At this point, her small inheritance provides her only means of future security. Because there are limited employment opportunities available to women in the public realm, neither Mary nor her counterparts in other seduction novels are encouraged or expected to assume a professional career. Mary certainly does not possess the same rights and privileges as do men of her race and class.

Although she is legally defined a *Feme Sole*, Mary's limited authority over her own person is clearly transient. Her only viable means of exercising authority over her life is to determine to which man she will give up her authority once she is married. To her family, Mary insists that, " . . . when I make [Haynes] master of my person, I shall also give him possession of my property and I trust he is of too generous a disposition ever to abuse my confidence" (ibid.). The story of Mary is a retelling of the seduction tales in Foster's *Boarding School*. These stories emphatically warn young republican women not to make impetuous marriage choices. Because she lacks critical skills and has been ill-prepared to confront her future, Mary rather imprudently makes an impetuous marriage choice (Rowson [1828] 1991, 179).

Consequently, Mary is seduced by Haynes into relinquishing her inheritances, her identity, and ultimately her body; she is the colonized woman. With this authority, Haynes, like his counterparts in *The Story of Margaretta* and *The Coquette*, eventually squanders Mary's inheritance and abandons her and their child. In a state of dejection, Mary painfully becomes aware of the reality of her tragic plight: "I am forsaken . . . deceived, plundered of fortune and good name. . . . I am more desolate than a widow; my infant . . . unless his father be led to do us justice, more wretched than an orphan" (ibid., 225). Subsequently, Mary and Frances Wellwood have no legal recourse, and even if they had, the stigma of the fallen woman would keep them ashamed and silent. Whether as a wife or daughter, a woman still has no recognizable voice under the law during this period; however, this does not suggest that because a woman is single, she is in a better position to voice her concerns. The narratives of seduction by Rowson quite realistically illustrate how a woman's voice can be easily usurped by those who thrive on wielding destructive, neocolonialist power over others.

In Rowson's seduction tales, a seduced or colonized woman loses her power to communicate. For instance, after she is abandoned to a state of poverty, Mary learns that her letters to the Matthews family were burned, as commanded by her seducer (ibid., 227). Of course, Charlotte Temple suffers a similar fate. Ann Douglas observes that the fallen woman shares the plight of the raped Philomel who suffered the ultimate form of silencing; that is, Philomel had her tongue cut out by her brother-in-law in order to prevent her from disclosing his identity as her rapist

(1991, xxxi). When Charlotte wants to send letters to her family, Montraville, concerned that he might be discovered, rips them to pieces and tosses them into the sea (ibid., 55). When Charlotte wants to send messages to Montraville after he leaves her at a New York cottage, Belcour orders a servant to steal her letters (ibid., 86). When both Montraville and Belcour appropriate Charlotte's voice, they appropriate her only viable means of communication; and subsequently, she is silenced as are many of her seduced and raped counterparts. In *Feminism and Philosophy*, Moira Gates observes that when women are reduced to silence, they become "locked in the body" (1991, 120). In this silent state, the body becomes the only viable means of communication, but the communication is effected through illness, depression, or madness. When Mrs. Beauchamp, Charlotte's neighbor, recognizes Charlotte's suffering, she intercedes by allowing Charlotte to mail letters to her parents in England. As a result, Charlotte's voice is restored enough to communicate her dying words to her parents. On some level, the stories of raped and silenced heroines that pervade the early nation's literature illustrate America's contributions to a long literary history portraying the rape and seduction of women. However, the narratives of seduction by Murray, Rowson, Tenney, and Foster clearly have educational and preventative agendas.

Within a sentimental frame, Mary, Frances, and Charlotte either have their stories narrated for them, or they are given a space to voice their own stories not only to prevent other women from suffering a similar plight but also to change the stigma of the fallen woman. Rowson's concern about the way a young woman handles her limited rights spurs Weil to conclude that Rowson was attempting to transform the perspectives of her audience. For the rights of women to be recognized by law, society has to change its attitudes about women, and Rowson's novels work endlessly toward this goal (Weil 1976, 60). When Mrs. Beauchamp reflects on Charlotte Temple, she senses the isolation and abandonment that a fallen woman must feel, but she also realizes that those who sympathize with the plight of the fallen endure condemnation as well. The narrator of *Charlotte Temple* tries to encourage bonds of friendship between women when she dramatically interrupts the text to address her audience:

> Believe me, many an unfortunate female, who has once strayed
> into the thorny paths of vice, would gladly return to virtue, was
> any generous friend to endeavor to raise and re-assure her; but
> alas! it cannot be, you say; the world would deride and scoff.
> Then let me tell you, Madam, 'tis a very unfeeling world. . . .
> (Rowson [1794] 1986, 68)

Through periodic interruptions of the story, the narrator attempts to
persuade her readers to accept her point of view about an issue. In this
instance, the narrator not only boldly champions the cause of the fallen
woman despite the social stigma, but she also condemns the world for
not bestowing kindness and charity upon the less fortunate. Defying the
traditional approach of shunning the fallen, Mrs. Beauchamp bestows
charity and compassion upon Charlotte (ibid., 74). By rejecting the conventional myth of the fallen woman, the friends of Mary and Frances also
refuse to acquiesce to tradition.

A reader of *Lucy Temple* and *Charlotte Temple* might assume the
position that Rowson is warning young women about how their declarations of independence can lead only to tragedy; however, this interpretation merits only limited support because of the subversive strain that
runs through the novels. In both *Charlotte Temple* and *Lucy Temple*, the
narrators emphasize that a single woman ill-prepared to meet life's complexity can experience tragedy. In both novels, the narrators also clearly
emphasize that the tragedies of Charlotte and Mary were consequences
of their mistaken education and a social system that fails to provide
them protection from fortune-hunters and profligates. In particular,
Charlotte's tragedy of being tossed into a hostile world is so intense that
the narrator is compelled to admit that a wife in an unhappy marriage
has at least the security of a home (ibid., 66). After Charlotte is abandoned by Montraville, she lives in poverty. Charlotte's food and shelter
must be provided by those willing to bestow charity.

In *Charlotte Temple*, the narrator emphasizes that even the pressuring of young women to marry old, wealthy men is nothing more than
legalized prostitution (ibid., 12). To avoid this and the tragedy of
Charlotte, a family should provide a young woman with a solid education
and an inheritance to protect her from arranged marriages and seduction (ibid.). A viable solution to this problem, though, appears to be
available only for the privileged woman with a substantial inheritance.

The story of Charlotte's daughter proves that this plan, for at least the privileged, is a success. Lucy Temple is the illegitimate daughter of Charlotte and Montraville. Throughout *Lucy Temple*, the narrator emphasizes that Lucy experienced the benefit of a well-rounded education. As a result, Lucy Temple, unlike Mary Lumley, Charlotte Temple, and Frances Wellwood, is astute, thoughtful, and knowledgeable of human behavior (Rowson [1828] 1991, 241). With these critical skills and a substantial inheritance, Lucy chooses to live an independent life dedicated to charity and the education of others. In a tribute to Lucy, the narrator exclaims:

> Her own education, her knowledge of human character and of nature, her cultivated and refined moral taste, and, above all, the healing and religious light, which her admirable submission to the trying hand of Providence had shed over the world and all its concerns as they appeared to her view,—all these things served to fit her for this species of ministry to the minds and hearts of these young persons. (ibid.)

In this particular passage, the narrator celebrates Lucy's choice to help others. With the religious undertones that pervade the passage, Lucy is portrayed as a Christlike figure who brings light into a world where darkness reigns. The narrator emphasizes that Lucy found the path to happiness and was amply rewarded for her goodness. Her presence in the world assisted many, including future generations who would benefit from her instruction because her students went on to educate others (ibid.). Like Rowson herself, Lucy contributed to the advancement of women's education and perhaps—the implication is—to women's advancement in religious vocations.

While conventional seduction narratives end with death and despair, *Lucy Temple* ends with hope. Although Rowson's posthumously published novel contains many of the conventional elements of the eighteenth-century narrative of seduction, it also proves to be a watershed that propels the sentimental novel into the nineteenth century with new visions for women's roles. When she allows Mary Lumley to be welcomed back into her family unit, Rowson disrupts the stigma of the fallen woman. When she allows the daughter of Charlotte Temple to live an independent adult life with a fulfilling and charitable career as an educator of other women, Rowson disrupts the stigmas of illegitimacy and spinsterhood.

Still further, Lucy's roles as an educator and minister to other women foreshadow women's activism in women's rights and religious reform. Indeed, when she draws a parallel between a woman and a minister, Rowson suggests that women, not just men, are capable of representing God on earth and that they, too, have instrumental roles to play in society.

Charlotte Temple and *Lucy Temple* help to transform the lives of middle- and upper-class women by offering alternative perspectives to women's traditional roles and expectations as well as to the stereotypes of the fallen woman. They offer, though, these alternative perspectives of women's lives only after they expose the profound turmoil a heroine endures when she is subjected to a social system that not only constricts her mind and body but also establishes her as a product of exchange between a father and a husband. When a woman contests her patriarchal status as property or as a medium of exchange, she is perceived as inviting conflict and consequently labeled a fallen woman.

This power struggle between the patriarchy and a young assertive woman manifests itself not only in Rowson's novels but in Tenney's *Female Quixotism* as well. In one episode, Mr. Sheldon asks his daughter to consult with him before accepting any marriage proposals, for she has a substantial inheritance to protect. At first, Dorcasina complies with her father's request; but when his demands become more persistent and her desire to marry Patrick O'Connor, a fortune-hunter, intensifies, she radically asserts her right to make her own decisions (Tenney [1801] 1992, 49). Indeed, a woman's declaration of independence in the face of patriarchal authority transforms her from a silent object to a speaking subject. Because of this transition in Dorcasina, Sheldon responds, "Alas! my daughter, how art thou fallen! You did not used to argue thus" (ibid.). Sheldon responds to his daughter's bold declaration of independence by labeling her a "fallen woman" not because she has formed a union with O'Connor but because she has defied patriarchal authority (ibid.).

Although seduction narratives emphasize power struggles between patriarchal authority and a young republican daughter, they also include struggles between a father and the daughter's seducer. Sheldon asks his daughter to reconsider marrying the rake, O'Connor, because he is an adventurer who recognizes Dorcasina as "the only child of a man of some property" (ibid., 48). Sheldon concludes that O'Connor wants "to gain possession of [Dorcasina's] heart, person and [her] father's estate" (ibid.). Thus, women such as Dorcasina Sheldon, Charlotte Temple, and Mary Lumley become the sites of a power struggle over property. The reduction of marriage to an economic exchange is illustrated further when another prospective suitor asks to marry Dorcasina. Dorcasina rejects Mr. Cumberland because of his impersonal treatment of her: "He has come here to make a bargain, as he calls it, just as if he had come to purchase an estate, without feeling for me" (ibid., 207). Certainly, Dorcasina boldly offers some rather perceptive insights about the function of women as commodities in her culture. Unlike some of her fallen counterparts, Dorcasina enters into neither a sexual relationship with a rake nor a marriage with a profligate, and, subsequently, she is able to retain her fortune. With this fortune, Dorcasina lives as a single woman with financial security.

Dorcasina's fallen counterpart in *The Coquette*, however, does not have the benefit of a substantial inheritance; consequently, she is discouraged from living as a single woman. Like the other narratives, Foster's *The Coquette* challenges both traditional, Puritanical views of the fallen woman and the viability of the middle-class woman's traditional status in the new republic. Foster bases her epistolary novel upon the scandalous story of Elizabeth Whitman, a Connecticut woman who died shortly after giving birth to a still-born child. In her introduction to *The Coquette*, Cathy Davidson notes that many journalists and ministers interpreting the Connecticut scandal used Whitman's story as the basis of a moral lesson in which they blamed everything from novel reading to her financial aspirations for her fall (1986, viii–ix). *The Coquette* is particularly fascinating because it links the protagonist's fall not with a deficient education or extensive novel reading but rather with the new nation's subduing of a woman's desire to embrace the unalienable rights of life, liberty, and the pursuit of happiness. In "Domesticating Virtue," Carroll Smith-Rosenberg observes that Eliza Wharton employs American Republican rhetoric throughout *The Coquette* to describe the extent to which she would like to determine her life (1988, 169).

The very opening of this epistolary novel reveals that Eliza is in a period of transition; she longs to break from traditions that restrict her movement and determine her life, just as the patriots longed to free themselves from colonialist oppression. In a letter to her friend Lucy Freeman, Eliza reveals her desire for freedom when she enthusiastically exclaims: "It is pleasure; pleasure . . . on leaving my paternal roof" (Foster [1797] 1986, 5). In "Signing as Republican Daughters: The Letters of Eliza Southgate and *The Coquette*," Irene Fizer explains that Eliza's opening exclamation indicates "a new realm of possibility. . . . she is testing out a new language . . . to accommodate her nascent sense of emancipation" (1993, 243–44). Fizer argues further that Eliza's desire to transcend her domestic realm reflects the sentiments felt by republican daughters of the era, such as Eliza Southgate, a student at Susanna Rowson's female academy (ibid., 246). Like Rowson's seduction novels, *The Coquette* marks a significant shift in the lives of republican women; that is, some women are questioning whether or not the sphere of domesticity can be completely fulfilling.

Although the American Revolution is over, the revolutionary fervor still pervades the nation and spurs some women to envision new roles for themselves in the new republic. Eliza's desires for emancipation and a new role hark back to her transformation after a period of mourning. In a letter to a friend, Eliza reveals that she felt for a time excluded from the world; and, in fact, she found herself, at times, "soaring above it" (Foster [1797] 1986, 7). At the opening of the novel, though, Eliza notes that she is beginning "to descend" (ibid.). After she emerges from a period of crisis, Eliza experiences a rebirth of energy and vitality.

This resurgence of energy and preoccupation with worldly concerns coincides with Eliza's willingness to relinquish practicing certain customs, for she has undergone a transformation of consciousness. A sign of her discontent with traditional customs is found in her denunciation of certain mourning rituals: "The absurdity of a custom, authorizing people at first interview to revive the idea of grief . . . is intolerable" (ibid., 90). Because she desires to lead a vivacious life, she rejects not only puritanical beliefs that label pleasure suspect but also "unthinking persons" who blindly comply with fashion and custom (ibid., 9). While she is probing, inquisitive, and logical, Eliza is also passionate about her invigoration. Eliza's acute understanding allows her to see beyond the boundaries of her world and recognize blind conformity to tradition. As a rational and emotional being, Eliza stands at the crossroads of waning Enlightenment thought and the emergence of the Romantic movement in Europe. Although she returns to worldly concerns, Eliza does so with an emergent and renewed sense of self.

Eliza's invigoration allows her to realize that she is on a new journey, a new path from which she will actively participate in the creation of her future. In her exploration of eighteenth-century political theory, Marguerite Fisher explains that the Enlightenment displaced the theory that human beings are subjected to predetermined character and life (1975, 40). Rather, life could be abundant with opportunity—the kind of opportunity that enthralls Eliza. Although she wants to determine her future, Eliza also realizes that there is a sense of uncertainty in her journey when she proclaims, in the closing of a letter, "Whatever my fate may be, I shall always continue your Eliza Wharton" (Foster [1797] 1986, 9). However, the new life Eliza chooses to embrace disrupts the traditional expectations of a woman of her class. From the perspectives of family and friends, Eliza openly invites conflict and, subsequently, tragedy. By the conclusion of the novel, the tensions between Eliza and her world violently erupt, and the effects manifest themselves on the sites of her mind, body, and spirit.

The system of social order of her day prevents Eliza from fully embracing individualism; thus, the primary cause of her downfall rests in her appropriation of the republican ideologies of freedom, independence, and self-determination that are not hers to appropriate. Throughout her correspondence, Eliza's language, whether literal or metaphorical, resonates with a desire for freedom and independence from the control of the paternal and the traditional. Because of economic and political factors, there were limited alternatives to marriage for eighteenth-century women (Cott 1977, 193). Since she has no significant inheritance, and regardless of her desire for freedom, Eliza is compelled to marry for economic security.

Eliza's appropriation of the rhetoric of the Declaration of Independence also threatens the very fabric of a male-dominated system that seeks to maintain its preeminence, in part, by relegating women to the domestic realm. In a letter to Lucy Freeman, Eliza expresses her sense of enslavement to patriarchal traditions when she proclaims:

I am young, gay, volatile. A melancholy event has lately extricated me from those shackles, which paternal authority had imposed on my mind. Let me have opportunity, unbiased by opinion, to gratify my natural disposition in a participation of those pleasures which youth and innocence afford (Foster [1797] 1986, 30).

Although Eliza's exultation reveals that her "mind" leads her to new directions, her friend, Mrs. Richman, believes that she follows the path of dissipation (ibid.). Mrs. Richman insists that Eliza misunderstands freedom and marriage. To this kind of policing mechanism, Eliza responds, "But I despise those contracted ideas which confine virtue to a cell" (ibid.). Because her choices and actions disrupt the traditional role of the middle-class woman, Eliza is labeled a coquette by her friends (ibid., 27).

In particular, Eliza's choice in the earlier part of the novel to remain single rouses condemnation from her friends because they believe the Reverend Boyer to be the most practical mate for her. Because of their disparity of dispositions, Eliza rejects Boyer, a prospective suitor. As a representative of Enlightenment rationalism who prides himself on being a practical and "reasonable creature," Boyer hardly constitutes a good marriage choice for Eliza who represents a balance between the logical and the emotional (ibid., 17). Claire Pettengill concludes that Eliza's unwillingness to commit immediately to marriage reflects "postrevolutionary anxieties, including issues of political alliance, economic change, social status, and urbanization" (1992, 186). Like Dorcasina Sheldon, Mary Lumley, and Margaretta Melworth, Eliza longs for a marriage that transcends the practical, for the practical represents the economical and the political. These heroines desire a marriage based upon love, trust, and equality—qualities they consider essential to wedded harmony and happiness. The conflicting views of marriage that arise in the novels represent the greater role women were demanding to play in determining their futures. In "Postmodernism or Postcolonialism Today," Simon During argues that victims of imperialism need "to achieve an identity uncontaminated by universalist or Eurocentric concepts and images" (1992, 125). All the fallen women met in the novels under review transcend—through desire or action—their prescribed roles. Because Eliza and Mary desire to determine their own lives, they demand to construct their own identities based upon their own principles, not the concepts and images superimposed upon them by a neocolonialist patriarchy represented by family and friends.

However, Eliza's choice to delay marriage and to pursue an independent life meets with harsh reproach; thus, she is falsely labeled by both men and women as a coquette. Represented as an astute, intelligent, and reflective woman, Eliza does desire to marry someday, but upon equal terms with an amiable husband. She hesitates to marry Reverend Boyer because she views his concept of her future realm of domesticity as boring, tedious, confining, and restrictive—an interesting critique of the "cult of domesticity" which claimed that women enjoyed sovereignty in their own homes. Although she thinks Boyer is amiable, Eliza recoils at forming an immediate connection with a man who will confine her "to the duties of domestic life" (Foster [1797] 1986, 29). If she enters into a union with Boyer, Eliza realizes that she will become "dependent for happiness, perhaps . . . for subsistence, upon a class of people, who will claim the right of scrutinizing every part of my conduct; and by censuring those foibles . . . may render me completely miserable" (ibid.). On some level, Eliza challenges those aspects of her world that oppress her. In "Decolonizing Culture," Ketu Katrak notes that women suffer from a "dual oppression" because "patriarchy that preceded and continues after colonialism . . . inscribes the concepts of womanhood, motherhood," and other traditions within an economic system (1995, 257). When she claims independence and the right to happiness as her own, Eliza challenges neocolonialist traditions. When she rejects traditional concepts of womanhood, she contests patriarchy. For Eliza, an unhappy marriage symbolizes slavery—an idea shared by Murray and Rowson's heroines. While she briefly agrees to an engagement with Boyer, Eliza gives consent only under the condition that she is not pressured into the actual union and, perhaps, even pregnancy. Eliza reveals: "However, I have compounded the matter with [Boyer], and conditioned that he shall expatiate on the subject, and call it by what name he pleases, platonic or conjugal, provided he will let me take my own time for the consummation" (Foster [1797] 1986, 66). Ultimately, *The Coquette* mirrors the growing disillusionment of some women with their prescribed roles and limited status in the new nation. Of course, this growing disillusionment sparks the process of the decolonization of women.

Another notable woman of the new republic who expressed sentiments similar to Eliza Wharton was Abigail Adams, America's first lady.
There is certainly ample evidence proving that Mercy Warren and Abigail
Adams were extremely concerned about the deliberate exclusion of
women's issues in the new laws that were to guide a nation into the next
century. In a letter (7 May 1776) to her husband, Abigail Adams expresses her outrage with legislators—including her husband—who deliberately
chose not to extend to women the rights that the patriots won:

> I cannot say that I think you very generous to the Ladies, for
> whilst you are proclaiming peace and good will to Men,
> Emancipating all Nations . . . you insist upon retaining an
> absolute power over wives. But you must remember that
> Arbitrary power is like most things which are very hard, very
> liable to be broken—notwithstanding all your wise Laws . . . we
> have it in our power not only to free ourselves but to subdue our
> Masters, and without violence throw both your natural and legal
> authority at our feet. (Rossi 1973, 13)

Heeding the sentiments expressed in America's Declaration of
Independence, Abigail Adams threatens yet another rebellion against
her husband and legislators if men's absolute control over their wives is
not dissolved. Abigail ardently believed that "all men would be tyrants if
they could" (ibid., 10). This bold declaration of independence by Abigail
confirms the deliberate legalization of women's subordinate status in the
new nation. It also reflects the privileged woman's evolving consciousness and desire to declare another war for independence; but this time,
the war is a civil one with members of the government. Perhaps Abigail
Adams' extensive correspondence with her friend, Mercy Warren, propelled her to so boldly remind her husband that the collective power of
women is strong enough to dissolve the political bands that subordinate
a wife to a husband and to alter a new government contrary to the interests of women.

Indeed, the dissatisfaction of Abigail Adams and Eliza Wharton with
their ascribed roles yields a critique of the "ideal" eighteenth- and nineteenth-century woman. In "The Cult of True Womanhood," Barbara
Welter describes the attributes that American society, from 1820–1860,

espoused as ideal in women; however, these characteristics also reflect the predominant expectations of privileged women during the late eighteenth century. As domestic beings, women were expected to represent piety, purity, and submissiveness to their fathers and husbands—characteristics that would deter women from declaring their independence. Women's reward for adhering to their ascribed lot would be future happiness (Welter 1966, 152). However, the narratives of seduction under review all disrupt such an expectation, for even if a woman marries an amiable husband, the marriage is not necessarily exempt of tragedy. As outspoken, active individuals, Eliza and Mary hardly want to take passive roles in the direction of their future.

Regardless of her desire for independence, if a woman did not exhibit piety and submissiveness, she was dubbed unnatural and unfeminine. When a woman chooses not to adhere to society's rigid standards of etiquette, society attempts to further block her freedom of expression and movement through stereotyping. Subsequently, these stereotypes encourage the relegation of fallen women to a lower order (ibid., 154). In particular, Boyer transforms his view of Eliza from an intelligent and caring woman to a scheming, deceitful coquette partly because he falls into a trap contrived by Sanford and partly because Eliza does not epitomize his patriarchal view of a "true woman" (Foster [1797] 1986, 78). In his position of religious authority, Boyer projects his notion of a woman's sole happiness upon Eliza; he ultimately fails to understand the reasons that compel Eliza to reject his perception of the "calm delights of domestic life" (ibid.). Because Eliza does not conform to his conventional concept of a woman, Boyer erroneously concludes that she possesses "false notions of happiness" (ibid.). To justify his hostile rejection of Eliza, Boyer claims that he was the victim of the "wiles of a deceitful girl" (78). In this position, Boyer projects his view of Sanford onto Eliza because she has chosen to associate with a profligate. Although Eliza's perceived deviance helps to emphasize her society's rigid rules and customs, her behavior also indicates the limited freedom her world offers a young republican woman seduced by the rhetoric of independence. Ironically, due to his seductive agenda, Sanford is the only individual of Eliza's circle who supports her choice to remain single and pursue her notion of happiness—a notion she has defined herself.

Like the works of Rowson and Tenney, Foster's novel imparts vital information to young readers who are entering the stage of their lives just before marriage. Mrs. Richman notices that Eliza experiences a tremendous amount of difficulty stepping into the next phase of her life. To help relieve some of Eliza's anxiety, Mrs. Richman claims that this transition period from a single life to marriage does not have to be filled with complexity when she proclaims, "How natural, and how easy the transition from one stage of life to another! Not long since I was a gay, volatile girl; seeking satisfaction in fashionable circles and amusements; but now I am thoroughly domesticated" (ibid., 97). For Eliza, though, the transition from one stage of life to the next is traumatizing, for she recognizes that the next stage of her life—the only socially acceptable option—is one filled with restriction and limitation. Marriage, as Eliza perceives it, symbolizes "the tomb of friendship" (ibid., 24). Eliza recognizes that if she subscribes to the life that is culturally imperative for her to assume—the realm of domesticity—she will suffer legal, spiritual, and psychological death. If she suffers a metaphorical death, Eliza cannot continue her journey of individuation. Although Mrs. Richman embraces her domestication, Eliza fights it just as the March sisters fight it a half century later in *Little Women*. Although she does desire to marry at some point, Eliza first wants to enjoy her sense of freedom. Interestingly, similar sentiments are expressed approximately seventy years later by Alcott herself—"for liberty is a better husband than love to many of us" (Chambers-Schiller 1984, 1).

In *Woman's Fiction*, Baym calls Eliza "a spoiled and artful flirt who refuses good marriage offers and dies disgraced in childbirth after she has succumbed to a seducer far more artful than she" (1978, 51). Eliza, however, is experiencing a distressing crisis with her marriage choices, and her indecisiveness and confusion reflect a much greater social problem. In effect, Eliza is a progressive thinker who envisions herself living in a world with unbounded freedom. With this freedom, Eliza could manifest her cerebral visions of her life's purpose—her desire to be self-determining and self-creating. Of course, as an active, thinking, feeling, and assertive woman, Eliza chooses to reject Calvinistic predestination, which maintains that an individual's life is predetermined; however, society dubs this rejection of predestination unacceptable for an eighteenth-century woman. Thus, Eliza's friends and relatives reject her progressive and visionary views of her life. This is not to suggest, though, that Eliza's desire for an independent life is particular only to her; Eliza's desire for a single life mirrors the sentiments of Lucy Temple and a few characters in Foster's *The Boarding School.*

Despite the social and political limits placed upon women, the novels being reviewed disrupt the myths of spinsterhood. In "Industry," Murray not only supports a woman's choice to remain single but also insists that society learn "to respect a single life, and even to regard it as the most eligible" unless a woman finds "a warm, mutual and judicious attachment" ([1797] 1992, 139). A single woman, argues Murray, should be respected whether that single life be a result of choice or circumstance; this entreaty, though, was still being articulated during the nineteenth century by Alcott in *Little Women*. A defense of spinsterhood also finds illustration in Tenney's *Female Quixotism* when the single life of a woman is deemed respectable and preferable to an unsuitable marriage ([1801] 1992, 76). In Foster's *The Boarding School*, Cleora Partridge, a graduate of Harmony Grove, invites her friend to remain single with her in order to dedicate themselves to the counsel of other women. Cleora insists that she could exemplify the success of a single life while concomitantly disproving the myths that single women are ill and odd (Foster 1798, 136–37).

In *The Coquette*, Eliza is discouraged from leading an independent life primarily because she lacks an inheritance; consequently, her desires to transcend the limitations and boundaries that thwart her freedom cannot yet be realized. Thus, she is inscribed as a deviant—a coquette. Throughout the novel, both men and women emphasize that Eliza benefited from an extensive education; however, that education has not been detailed. Although Foster's *The Boarding School* and the novels by Rowson, Murray, and Tenney draw a link between seduction and education, this link in *The Coquette* is not substantiated. Throughout her correspondence, Eliza demonstrates intelligence and reflection. Julia Granby notes that Eliza possesses the ability to detect and repel profligates; Eliza possesses the benefits of an education, knowledge of the world and human behavior, and a thorough understanding of Sanford as a libertine who would "deceive and betray her" (Foster [1797] 1986, 145). While, clearly, she is the object of Sanford's scheming and vengeful seduction, Eliza succumbs because of depression catalyzed by her sense of restriction. Through the policing actions of her friends, Eliza learns that her desire to lead the life of her choice is socially unacceptable, particularly when she is repeatedly made aware of the fact that she lacks an inheritance. Eliza meets with hostility and condemnation from family and friends, who finally provide some understanding of her plight only after she willingly leaves her home in disgrace.

The Coquette is not a bildungsroman that traces the educational or spiritual development of the protagonist from youth to adulthood. However, it does trace the physical, spiritual, and psychological decline of a young woman caught at the crossroads between a traditional way of life that no longer fulfills a republican daughter and a space—a way of life—that still needs prefiguring. Indeed, *The Coquette* documents a number of crises experienced by Eliza, one of which is a philosophical crisis. On the one hand, when she opts to reject predestination, she boldly chooses to base her life choices upon free will (ibid., 24). On the other hand, Eliza's social circle will not foster or support a young middle-class woman with no inheritance who chooses to direct her own life. In particular, Lucy Freeman castigates her friend for longing to be upwardly mobile, for Eliza's "situation in life is, perhaps, as elevated as [she has] a right to claim" (ibid., 27).

Eliza's succumbing to seduction represents, in part, a self-fulfilling prophesy. Eliza's family and friends believe that she has fallen long before she enters into a sexual relationship with Sanford, and, indeed, she internalizes this perspective. To help illuminate the intensity of her fallen status, spatial metaphors are used throughout the text by Eliza and her family; but the metaphors emphasize the vertical position of Eliza's journey (her "fall") rather than her desire for a horizontal path of progression leading toward her future. When she "descends" to meet Sanford within her home, Eliza is both psychologically devastated and physically emaciated. Because she defies traditions that determine the life of a middle-class woman with no inheritance, Eliza falls, as David Waldstreicher argues, under "the gaze of others" (1992, 207). Indeed, Eliza, like her counterparts in other American seduction novels, cries the traditional lament, "I am undone," long before her seduction by Sanford (Foster [1797] 1986, 105). In addition to an inadequate education, a woman's dubious political status in the new nation makes her economically, physically, and psychologically vulnerable to seduction.

The Coquette shares many concerns over seduction and the status of the *Feme Sole* and the *Feme Covert* with the novels by Rowson, Murray, and Tenney; it also shares with them the plan to raise the consciousness of the American fair. *The Coquette* acts as a guide for the middle-class woman confronting, perhaps, the most pivotal decision of her life—marriage. Like *Charlotte Temple, The Coquette* imparts vital information to young women about the complexity of life. Life is a moral trial filled with obstacles that present some lesson that must be learned in order to move on to the next stage of personal growth and development. "Past experience will point out the quicksand which you are to avoid in your future course," explains Lucy Sumner to Eliza (ibid., 108). "Our greatest mistakes may teach lessons which will be useful through life" explains Mrs. Richman to the pained Eliza (ibid., 97). While Lucy Sumner and Mrs. Richman attempt to persuade Eliza to view her encounter with Sanford as a learning experience that could help guide her future conduct and choices, they fail to address or understand the complexity of her crisis. The lesson that needs to be taught is that the new nation has to transform its views of women in order for women to survive the next century.

By exposing the double standard and the injustice of a new nation that claims that only a select group of individuals are endowed with unalienable rights, *The Coquette* disrupts and displaces the dominant ideologies and paradigms that construct the lives of women. In a sense, Rowson's drama, *Slaves in Algiers*, most overtly reinforces the messages of the seduction novels in question when it reminds the new nation that the struggle for freedom abandoned women. In particular, Fetnah, an outspoken Moroccan woman living under the rule of her father, Ben Hassan, in Algiers, is informed rather ironically by an American woman who became the Algerian captive of Hassan that "woman was never formed to be the abject slave of man. Nature made us equal with them, and gave us the power to render ourselves superior" (Rowson 1794, 9). Invigorated by her new understanding of independence, Fetnah vows: "I was born free, and while I have life, I will struggle to remain so" (ibid.). All the narratives of seduction in consideration expose the fundamental problems confronting women in their struggle for freedom. The clash between the traditional view of woman as the "weaker sex" and the astute understanding that gender and class influenced the creation of a new nation erupts in the form of seduction.

The seduction narratives under evaluation explore the root causes of women's status as the weaker sex and the consequent legalization of women's inequality. Murray's writings, in particular, are cultural critiques that seek to transform the power relations between men and women. Both Murray and Rowson recognize gender as the basis for the organization of society, for the construction of female and male identities, and for ways of making sense of reality. By articulating and exposing gender role differences that patriarchy requires, the novels under review disclose the biased, misogynous myths that govern women's lives. After the American Revolution, America was concentrating on the building of a new nation. Both Murray and Rowson believed that this nation could not be truly democratic unless women were part of the restructuring process and their rights as citizens were recognized. The key to reforming women's status in the new republic was to change women's subordinate place in society—beginning with legal and educational reform. In fact, Foster also challenges individuals who oppose a female's participation in the political process when, in *The Coquette*, Mrs. Richman fearlessly asserts that women have the right to discuss politics: "We think ourselves interested in the welfare and prosperity of our country; and, consequently claim the right of inquiring into those affairs, which may conduce to, or interfere with the common wealth" (Foster [1797] 1986, 44). Mrs. Richman and Eliza Wharton realize that they are prevented from serving in the senate, but this will not prevent them from expressing their concern about the well-being of the young nation. Although Mrs. Richman is applauded as truly republican, her liberating views about a woman's right to discuss politics are a significant part of the decolonization of women (ibid.).

Yet, before women could embark on the journey for independence, the fallacies that prevented them from being independent had to be exposed and shattered. In her radical political tract, "On the Equality of the Sexes" (1790), Murray not only joins the ongoing political and philosophical debates of her day but also sets out to rebut the popular notions of the Enlightenment by employing the same tools as the most preeminent European philosophers of the eighteenth century—the same philosophers whose thoughts to varying degrees inspired the creators of the Declaration of Independence. Rousseau, Locke, Hobbes, and religious enthusiasts use nature as the vantage point from which to determine the legal space of men and women; Murray, too, explores women's place in a state of nature. As a leading political theorist of democracy, Rousseau wrote an essay (1754) in which he pondered, "What is the origin of inequality among men, and is it authorized by natural law." Murray, in "On the Equality of the Sexes," explores the genesis of woman's presumed inequality with man, and explains that it is not authorized by natural law:

> Is it upon mature consideration we adopt the idea, that nature is thus partial in her distributions? Is it indeed a fact that she hath yielded to one half of the human species so unquestionable a mental superiority? I know that to both sexes elevated understanding, and the reverse, are quite common. But, suffer me to ask; in what the minds of females are so notoriously deficient, or unequal? (1790, 132)

For many eighteenth-century political theorists and religious zealots, women were created—in a state of nature or in the garden of Eden—inferior to men. From this premise many Enlightenment thinkers build their arguments for social and familial structuring. However, after "mature consideration," Murray disrupts this premise by suggesting that this theory of woman as the weaker sex is neither logical nor sound. There is nothing enlightening about Enlightenment thought or its use of reason when it comes to its superstitious view of women. Murray actually dares to call into question the governing premise that has structured civilization since Biblical times. Murray does not argue against the hierarchical structure that places God as the supreme ruler over nature, but rather, she argues against man's purported natural physical and intellectual superiority to woman.

While Murray does embrace certain facets of Enlightenment thought, she recognizes the inherent danger of misusing reason to posit egocentrically based political beliefs that fail to benefit all. Murray and her literary contemporaries had to contend with traditional individuals who were aligned with the misogyny of Rousseau. Cott notes that many objections to female improvement in the new republic could, in fact, be traced back to Rousseau (1977, 110). In his novel *Emile*, Rousseau purports: "Women do wrong to complain of the inequality of man-made laws; the inequality is not of man's making, or at any rate it is not the result of mere prejudice, but of reason" ([1762] 1972, 324). Rousseau's novel provides his most comprehensive misogynist insights on women's rights and education. For Rousseau and many of his predecessors, women were born for dependence and servitude (Fisher 1975, 40). In the epilogue of *Slaves in Algiers*, Rowson boldly asserts her indignation toward traditionalists when she exclaims to the female members of her audience that "Women were born for universal sway/ Men to adore, be silent, and obey" (1794, 73).

Of course, the view of women as the inferior sex was adopted by the founding fathers of the new nation. Murray's thoughts not only reflect the radical ideas of some of her countrywomen who are part of an unofficial counterculture, but they also disrupt the conventional theories of her age that contend women lack reason and intelligence. As a member of the political realm, John Adams, in particular, perpetuates the traditional notion that women lack reason and judgment when he informs a friend about his rationale preventing women and men who did not own property from voting:

> . . . generally speaking women and children have as good judg-
> ments, and as independent minds, as those men who are wholly
> destitute of property; these last being . . . as much dependent
> upon others, who will please to feed, clothe, and employ them,
> as women are upon their husbands, or children on their parents.
> (Rossi 1973, 15)

In other words, women were akin in status to men without property, for propertyless men ultimately failed to demonstrate good judgment and independence. Subsequently, the myths that women were irrational and incompetent kept them legally subordinate and dependent upon husbands and fathers. As further revealed in the correspondence of John Adams, an individual's right to vote in the new republic was determined not only by gender but by class and race.

In *Women of the Republic*, Kerber concludes that Murray, Rowson, and Foster were among many notable eighteenth-century women who contributed to the formation of not only a new female ideology but a new era in female history (1980, 11). In "Industry," Murray boldly asserts that she would give her daughter and the daughters of the new nation every accomplishment open to their brothers ([1797] 1992, 139). But in order for women to prepare for this new journey, they need the skills to procure for themselves the necessities of life. "Independence," argues Murray, "should be placed within [women's] grasp; and I would teach them to reverence themselves" (ibid.).

Murray's declaration of women's independence was quite radical for the 1790s in New England when Puritanism and Calvinism still pervaded the fabric of the nation. However, the concept of independence shared by these four authors was still quite different from the independence enjoyed by property owners who had the right to vote, sign contracts, and attend college. These four writers encouraged their readers to educate their daughters not only about mathematics and science but about their rather dubious status in the new nation. For Murray, female independence meant self-reliance. However, before a woman could demonstrate self-reliance, she needed to develop self-esteem and self-respect. The social and political climate of the late eighteenth century would not allow much more than this, but self-reliance was, indeed, the first step in a long journey women were to embark upon in the attainment of rights and independence. Most certainly, Murray's passionate essays were published during a time when many did not want to upset the status quo socially, politically, or philosophically; but this did not deter Murray, Foster, Tenney, or Rowson from further voicing their views on the origins of female inequality in their narratives of seduction.

Although the "dye" has been cast for Charlotte Temple, Eliza Wharton, and Mary Lumley, the inevitable journey of tragedy that follows need not claim any more women if young readers allow their psyches to be transformed by the lessons imparted in the seduction novels under consideration. Carl Jung wrote that the social significance of art and literature lies in the education of "the spirit of the age, conjuring up the forms in which the age is most lacking" (1978, 82). The recurrent themes of women's seduction and political disenfranchisement perhaps remind the new nation that its neocolonization of women reverts to a way of life America arduously desired to escape. Throughout the novels under review, the seduced woman represents not only the legal system's failure to protect the rights of women, but also the nation's failure to include women in its declaration of freedom and independence. However, the narratives in question also transcend the political by voicing the silent suffering invisible to the public realm; that is, the silent suffering and desperation experienced by a republican daughter abandoned by her new nation.

3

Seduction and Neocolonization:
The Presence of a Rape Culture

I𝖭 *Transforming Rape Culture*, Emilie Buchwald, Pamela Fletcher, and Martha Roth define "rape culture" as "a complex set of beliefs that encourages male sexual aggression and supports violence against women. A rape culture condones physical and emotional terrorism against women as the norm" (1993, Preamble). In order to eradicate the conditions that foster rape and other violent acts against women, "a revolution of values," the editors argue, must take place (ibid., 2). What is particularly fascinating about the narratives of Rowson, Foster, Murray, and Tenney is that they represent not only the characteristics of a rape culture during the early national period but also the need to revolutionize traditional perspectives on seduction and rape. As consciousness-raising devices, the narratives of seduction by these four writers help young middle- and upper-class women better prepare themselves for their futures in the new republic. These seduction narratives impart valuable lessons to their audiences about the importance of a well-balanced education and promote an awareness of the rather dubious laws that constrict the lives of women.

Of course, these lessons all center around the act of seduction. In the novels under review, seduction involves the use of lies, false pretenses, and psychological intimidation to induce a woman into marriage or sexual relations. When a seducer persuades a woman into marriage, he wants to gain access to both her inheritance and her body. These novels emphasize that a woman is vulnerable to seduction not only because of her limited education and legal rights but also because the culture in which she dwells fosters a rapist ethic and a neocolonialist attitude.

Representative of a rapist ethic and a neocolonialist perspective, Richardson's Lovelace serves as the prototype for the seducers met in many American seduction narratives. When he declares his motives for raping Clarissa, Lovelace reveals: "I have three passions that sway me by turns; all imperial ones. Love, revenge, ambition, or a desire of conquest" (Richardson [1747-8] 1962, 261). In actuality, Lovelace's neocolonialist approach to life and his relationship with Clarissa intersect with many other perspectives. Quite literally, Lovelace, Sanford from the *The Coquette*, O'Connor in *Female Quixotism*, and other seducers met in the novels internalize and practice the colonialist endeavors of England, Spain, and other countries; however, their desires to possess, conquer, and violate are reenacted upon the female body, particularly the young female body.

Indeed, colonizers and seducers practice their "ordained roles." In Genesis, man is created to subdue and to dominate the earth and all its inhabitants. Colonialist and rapist views can trace their roots back to a passage in Genesis—"Be fruitful and multiply, and fill the earth and subdue it; and have dominion over . . . every living thing that moves upon earth" (1:29). Embraced by the Western world, the biblical creation myth provides the foundation for man's egocentric world view. Resurrected and perpetuated by the Enlightenment, this Biblical passage also served to validate man's scientific and rational approaches to conquering nature and the world. By revealing the profiles and agendas of seducers and representing how victims suffer the consequences of seduction, the novels of Murray, Foster, Rowson, and Tenney expose the perspectives that fuel a rapist ethic and its ability to thrive in a rape culture.

Among the narratives of seduction by these four writers that epitomize the rapist ethic detailed by John Stoltenberg and Rus Funk, *The Coquette* offers the most comprehensive psychological profile of a seducer who systematically sets out to stalk and violate a woman. Throughout an epistolary correspondence, Peter Sanford relates his private thoughts about women and the woman he seduces to his friend, Charles Deighton. Through this correspondence, readers learn the neocolonialist perspectives of rape and war that Sanford projects on his reality. When he is introduced in the text, Sanford informs Deighton that he has met Eliza Wharton. If Eliza proves to be a coquette, that is, a woman who does not immediately reject him, Sanford will establish an oppositional relationship with her. On some level, Sanford believes that if a woman acts coquettishly, she is automatically at war with man. This presumption reflects Sanford's belief that he possesses the tacit right to vindicate mankind. To his friend, Sanford boasts: "I shall avenge my sex, by retaliating the mischiefs [Eliza] mediates against us. Not that I have any ill designs; but only to play off her own artillery, by using a little unmeaning gallantry. And let her be aware of the consequences" (Foster [1797] 1986, 18). Thus far, Eliza has shared only conversation and dancing with Sanford at a gathering. After this one brief meeting, Sanford fabricates an assessment of Eliza that is deeply imbricated upon his misogyny and warlike attitude.

In *Against Our Will: Men, Women and Rape*, Susan Brownmiller explains that historically rape has been a consequence of war and imperialist pursuits. According to Brownmiller, war provides "the perfect psychologic backdrop" for men "to give vent to their contempt for women"; often, war provides men with a "tacit license to rape" (1975, 33). In instances of war, rape becomes an effective way to exert power over the opposition; that is, raping the women of adversaries is akin to violating the property of adversaries. For individuals embracing a neocolonialist perspective, rape means scoring and conquering (ibid., 35). In "Theory and Practice: Pornography and Rape," Robin Morgan also argues, "The violation of an individual woman is the metaphor for man's forcing himself on whole nations (rape as the crux of war), on nonhuman creatures (rape as the lust behind hunting and related carnage), and on the planet itself" (1977, 169). Rape and seduction are the culmination of an individual's desire to subdue, conquer, and dominate.

Like his prototype Lovelace, Sanford longs to fulfill his desires to subdue and conquer. With a neocolonialist attitude, Sanford declares an unofficial war against the opposite sex; but this is a war that he fabricates and projects onto his world. Throughout his correspondence, Sanford emphasizes that he loves Eliza, but because she lacks an inheritance and he lacks an income, he chooses not to marry her. Since he will not "possess" her entirely through marriage, Sanford refuses to allow Eliza to be the "property of another" (Foster [1797] 1986, 35). As a scheming strategist, Sanford endeavors to separate Eliza from Reverend Boyer not only because, if unattached, she would be far more easy to seduce into a sexual relationship but also because he "loves" her "too well to see her connected with another for life" (ibid., 56). After he reduces Eliza to her legal equivalent, a piece of property, Sanford deliberately sets out to damage her chastity and reputation, and, subsequently, her economic worth on the marriage market. Sanford's use of war and game metaphors serves to emphasize further his oppositional relationship with Eliza; however, it also serves as a reflection of his psychological profile and his way of interpreting his external environment.

For instance, in a letter to his friend, Sanford confesses that he has additional motives for scheming against Eliza:

> I must own myself a little revengeful too in this affair. I wish to punish her friends, as she calls them, for their malice towards me; for their cold and negligent treatment of me whenever I go to the house. I have not yet determined to seduce her. . . . And if I should, she can blame none but herself, since she knows my character, and has no reason to wonder if I act consistently with it. (ibid.)

As an opportunist, Sanford systematically sets out to seduce Eliza not only because of the thrill of conquering her for one moment of pleasure but because he also seeks revenge against her friends and family for rejecting him. As the novel progresses, Sanford's jealousy and desire to damage Eliza intensifies, particularly when she engages other prospective suitors in conversation. As a result, Sanford desires to seek revenge against not only Eliza but also those who associate with her. Motivated by his lust, his desire to avenge, and his desire to conquer, Sanford epitomizes an American Lovelace.

As an American Lovelace, Sanford projects an attitude that signifies his sense of superiority and his confidence in his ability to carry out his plans. His sense of superiority reflects his belief that he possesses the necessary characteristics to persuade and lure women from the use of reason. To his friend, Sanford reveals his plans to achieve a victory in the unofficial war between the sexes: "Our entrapping a few of their sex only discovers the gaiety of our dispositions, the insinuating graces of our manners, and the irresistible charms of our persons and address" (ibid., 55). A charming, handsome, and charismatic facade provides the means by which seducers prevail. Although Sanford's plan reveals the devices seducers use to entrap women, it also reveals seducers as astute, confident, and manipulative individuals who premeditate their acts of seduction.

Confident of his ability to seduce Eliza, Sanford boasts of his power over her. In a letter to his friend, Sanford admits that, if he so chooses, he can access Eliza's body: "Well, Charles, the show is over, as we Yankees say; and the girl is my own. That is, if I will have her. I shall take my own time for that, however. I have carried my point, and am amply revenged on the whole posse of those dear friends of hers. . . . Thank God I have no conscience" (ibid., 94–95). Because he assumes a superior position and claims to have no morals, he realizes that he has reduced Eliza to a submissive position; thus, he can colonize her mind and her body.

Although he projects a confident and manipulating facade, there are moments in which Sanford is at war with his emotions. When he first meets Eliza, Sanford perceives her to be a coquette at war with men. After he becomes acquainted with her, he admits that Eliza exemplifies a good and kind person who would make an excellent wife (ibid., 23). This change in perspective, though momentary, poses deep turmoil for Sanford. Because he has squandered his fortune, Sanford chooses to marry only a woman with a substantial inheritance (ibid.). Despite his misogynistic views of women, Sanford recognizes Eliza's sincerity and goodness, but he feels out of control when he states that he does not mean "to abuse her credulity and good nature, if I can help it" (ibid.). From a colonialist and a patriarchal perspective, Sanford dichotomizes women. Women are either coquettes or angels. In many eighteenth-century sentimental novels, seducers appear to possess an innate desire to corrupt the innocent and to prey upon the most vulnerable as a reaffirmation of their power. A seducer's choice to prey upon the most vulnerable reflects his inability to exert power in other aspects of his life. Because they are unable to secure professional incomes, Sanford, Courtland, and O'Connor choose to pursue women with inheritances. Although he cannot marry Eliza for financial gain, Sanford still uses her as a site over which he can fulfill his need for dominance. Even though he claims that he has neither morals nor a conscience, Sanford recognizes his seduction of Eliza as an act of revenge. Indeed, it is a hate crime. When he claims that he has no conscience, Sanford attempts to justify his evasion of responsibility for his actions. Because he realizes, on some level, that his desire to seduce Eliza is immoral and malicious, Sanford momentarily entertains some doubts about seducing her; however, he ultimately refuses to negotiate or relinquish his imperial pursuits. He remains loyal to the characteristics that define him as a seducer.

Of all the heroines met in the novels under review, Eliza Wharton recognizes the most clearly that she is the object of a seducer's desire. In a letter to a friend, Eliza admits that her heart is "again besieged" (ibid., 24). Of course, she recognizes Sanford as the assailant. In the beginning of the novel, though, Eliza has not yet determined whether or not she will surrender: "I am unable at present to determine. Sometimes I think of becoming a predestinarian, and submitting implicitly to fate, without any exercise of free will" (ibid.). Concerned about her friend's well-being, Mrs. Richman warns Eliza about Sanford's resemblance to Lovelace. Mrs. Richman fears that if Eliza does not terminate her companionship with Sanford, she will become another Clarissa. Eliza, though, objects to Mrs. Richman's perspective and exclaims, "I hope, madam, you do not think me an object of seduction!" (ibid., 38). In response, Mrs. Richman claims that, "I do not think you seducible; nor was Richardson's Clarissa, till she made herself the victim, by her own indiscretion" (ibid.). Because Sanford demonstrates an artful and conniving mannerism, Mrs. Richman fears that, like Clarissa, Eliza will be harmed.

Like preceptress Williams of *The Boarding School* and, perhaps, even the mythic Circe, Mrs. Richman advises Eliza to deafen her ears to Sanford's "syren voice of flattery" (ibid.). With her allusion to Greek myth, Mrs. Richman forewarns Eliza about the siren-like qualities possessed by Sanford, whose passionate rhetoric and uninhibited actions can lead young women to their doom. Of course, Sanford's acute rhetoric also resonates with the rhetoric of Biblical Satan who assumes the guise of a snake in the Garden of Eden. In a particular letter, Eliza recounts a conversation she had with Sanford in which he revealed that he had been trying to arrange a meeting with her. In this conversation, Sanford claims he tried to contact her earlier, but since he could not reach her, he decided to visit her in person. When he learns that Eliza is not in her home but rather in her "garden," Sanford takes "the liberty to invade her retirement" (ibid., 37). Sanford not only possesses the characteristics of Greek sirens but also those of a Satan who invades Eliza's Garden of Eden.

On another level, Eliza recognizes that Boyer also has the power to seduce her. In a letter to Lucy Freeman, Eliza notes that Boyer may be desirous of seducing her into marriage, and, indeed, he is "very eloquent upon the subject" (ibid., 66). In a letter to his friend, Boyer admits that he does plan to persuade Eliza into marriage (ibid., 11, 16); his seduction of Eliza, though, is motivated not by financial gain nor a desire to attain her for sexual pleasure only. Rather, Boyer desires to marry Eliza for practical reasons and rational principles. As a representative of Enlightenment rationalism, Boyer believes that Eliza would make a kind, intelligent, attractive wife for a minister (ibid., 10).

Throughout *The Coquette*, both men and women view courtship as a game that requires the victor to have a well-planned strategy. Indeed, the courtship process and the political environment of the late eighteenth century mirror each other because they both make a young woman vulnerable to fortune-hunters and profligates. Eliza, too, admits that she adorns herself "for a new conquest" at her frequent social gatherings (ibid., 62). Even though Eliza participates actively in courtship rituals, she is certainly casual and playful in her use of the term "conquest." She is operating far from the base on which Sanford utters and, in fact, implements the terminology. Although she may claim that she puts off marriage, in part, until she has "sowed all [her] wild oats" (ibid., 68), Eliza does not practice this behavior. The correspondence between friends in *The Coquette* reveals not only the complex way a man and a woman objectify each other in the courtship process, but also the complex way a man and a woman interpret and misinterpret each other's actions. Ultimately, such courtship rituals support acquaintance rape.

Sanford's misinterpretation of Eliza reflects not only his neocolonialist perspective but also the rapist ethics that determine his behavior. In *Refusing to be a Man*, Stoltenberg explains that rapists often project their sense of responsibility onto the women they have raped (1990, 19). For instance, Sanford justifies his seduction of Eliza not only by insisting that she is a coquette, an energetic woman who seeks happiness and dares to speak with other men at social gatherings, but also by blaming her for his crime. He rationalizes Eliza's responsibility in the seduction by insisting that she was aware of his intentions: " . . . If I should [seduce her], she can blame none but herself, since she knows my character . . ." (Foster [1797] 1986, 56). After he seduces Eliza and his wife sues him for divorce, Sanford considers marrying Eliza; however, he soon dismisses this prospect because Eliza is so "seducible" (ibid., 157). This double standard is illustrated also in *Charlotte Temple*. Belcour attempts to convince Montraville not to accept any personal responsibility for Charlotte's tragedy. Through his misogynistic rationalizations, Belcour suggests that if Montraville could seduce Charlotte then any man could do so (Rowson [1794] 1986, 83). Belcour blames Charlotte for her tragedy just as Sanford blames Eliza for hers. When Sanford learns that Eliza's family and friends accuse him of being a vicious seducer, he reaffirms his vengeful motives: "I always swore revenge for their dislike and coldness towards me" (Foster [1797] 1986, 158). According to Stoltenberg, before a man sexually assaults a woman, he constructs her as a sexual target. The stereotyping of women allows some rapists to justify their crimes, and objectification allows them to depersonalize their contact with their victims (Stoltenberg 1990, 54). Sanford's objectification of Eliza allows him to misread her and, subsequently, to establish an oppositional relationship with her. Sanford assumes that Eliza understands his personality and thus tacitly consents to sexual relations (Foster [1797] 1986, 56). In other words, Sanford believes that Eliza is "asking for" her seduction.

On another level, however, Sanford realizes his seduction of Eliza is a crime. Once he achieves his goal of seducing Eliza, Sanford boasts to his friend that he has encountered "a long and tedious siege," but "stolen waters" are the best (ibid., 139). Even though Sanford speaks metaphorically of his seduction of Eliza, he clearly understands that he has violated her: she is "stolen waters." As he brags about his conquest, Sanford explains the scene he initially envisioned sharing with Eliza. He assumed that Eliza would participate in the seduction: "Indeed, I should have given over the pursuit long ago, but for the hopes of success I entertained from her parleying with me, and in reliance upon her own strength, endeavoring to combat, and counteract my designs" (ibid., 140). As a member of the dominant group, Sanford describes Eliza in terms derived from his misogynistic perspective. He projects his views and expectations of all women onto Eliza. Although he admits that he should have relinquished his pursuit of her, Sanford chooses to remain faithful to the challenge and his neocolonialist desires. Eliza's unwillingness to immediately commit herself to Sanford poses a challenge for him; thus, gaining access to her body signifies his long-awaited victory and his ability to subdue and conquer. This kind of challenge, argues Stoltenberg, provides a rapist with the ultimate test of his masculinity (1990, 79). Throughout the narratives under consideration, seduction is portrayed not only as a premeditated crime but also as an act that represents war and combat. In *The Coquette*, the intersection between rape and neocolonialism becomes clear.

The connection between colonialism and seduction manifests itself also in *Charlotte Temple*. Like many other profligates met in seduction narratives, Montraville dons a handsome, charismatic, and persuasive facade. At one point in *Charlotte Temple*, the narrator emphasizes that "Montraville was tender, eloquent, ardent, and yet respectful" (Rowson [1794] 1986, 38). Indeed, this charm allows Montraville to persuade Charlotte, whom he had met at a dance prior to the opening of the novel, into clandestine meetings. Montraville's handsome appearance spurs the narrator of *Charlotte Temple* to interrupt the story to forewarn her young audience directly about the dangers of soldiers. In a maternal voice, the narrator explains that British soldiers have a particular style that adds to their dashing appeal: "When beauty of person, elegance of manner, and an easy method of paying compliments, are united to the scarlet coat, smart cockade, and military sash, ah! well-a-day for the poor girl who gazes on him: she is in imminent danger" (ibid., 28). What kind of danger awaits a young, naive girl with a deficient education? Throughout the novel, Montraville, like Sanford, consciously and strategically sets out to seduce Charlotte into a sexual relationship in which he will assume no responsibility for his actions until after her death.

Although she is, at first, attracted to Montraville, Charlotte grows fearful of him when he continues to pressure her into clandestine meetings. At one meeting, Charlotte becomes so frightened by his insistence on meeting that she finds herself "struggling to draw her hands from him" (ibid., 39). Although Montraville dons a charismatic air, his relationship with Charlotte is immediately established as oppositional. On some level, Charlotte feels the need to escape from him (ibid.). During their meetings, Montraville emphasizes that he is a soldier who will be embarking on a mission to America. Because he insists that he may never see her again, Montraville begs Charlotte to depart to America with him, his friend Belcour, and her teacher La Rue. "And what end he proposed to himself by continuing the acquaintance he had commenced with [Charlotte]," the narrator ponders, "he did not at that moment give himself time to enquire" (ibid., 41). Although he realizes that he deceives Charlotte, Montraville's speeches become more intense and persuasive. At one point, Charlotte momentarily consents to elope with Montraville but only under the condition that he fulfill his promise of marriage. In fact, Charlotte pleads with Montraville not to renege on this promise. A power struggle exists not only between Montraville and Charlotte but also indirectly between Montraville and Charlotte's parents. Charlotte recognizes that she is bound to her parents for protection and support. Keenly aware of this bond, Montraville convinces Charlotte to sever the relationship with her parents and attach herself to him for protection. Charlotte reminds Montraville that if he should renege on this engagement, she will be abandoned on "a foreign shore" (ibid., 43). Indeed, he has no intention of marrying Charlotte, yet Montraville falsely promises her that they will be legally united in America (ibid., 44).

Although she momentarily consents to go to America with Montraville, Charlotte alters her decision and informs Montraville of this change. While there may appear to be grounds supporting the formation of an oral contract since both an offer and acceptance have been negotiated between Montraville and Charlotte, Charlotte theoretically still belongs to her father and has no recognizable legal standing; thus, she cannot make oral contracts. Of course, Belcour and La Rue hardly make credible witnesses, especially when they act as accomplices in Montraville's seduction of Charlotte.

In "The American Novel of Seduction," Mona Scheuermann argues that the acts in *Charlotte Temple* are not seductions because Charlotte "consents to run off with her soldier [who] does not kidnap or rape her" (1978, 111). However, the scenes leading up to Charlotte's departure with Montraville prove quite the contrary. After reflection, Charlotte informs Montraville that "religion and duty" forbid her to go with him to America (Rowson [1794] 1986, 47). Although Charlotte clearly and formally rejects him, Montraville's arguments become more intense. He even threatens to commit suicide if Charlotte does not elope with him to America: "If you disappoint my ardent hopes, by all that is sacred, this hand shall put a period to my existence. I cannot—will not live without you" (ibid.). By preying upon her fear, naivete, and innocence, Montraville misleads Charlotte. An authority figure's manipulation of a young girl is hardly a basis for a consensual sexual relationship.

Because of Montraville's incessant pleas and false promises, Charlotte is under a considerable amount of duress. In a moment of confusion, she exclaims: "How shall I act" (ibid.). At this point, Montraville usurps Charlotte's power to reason by insisting, "Let me direct you." As he appropriates Charlotte's decision-making power, he also restrains her power of movement by seizing her and putting her into the chaise. An argument for abduction certainly can be formulated. After Montraville seizes her, Charlotte cries out that her parents have been forsaken. Overwhelmed by these events, Charlotte faints (ibid., 48). When she reaches the shores of America, Charlotte realizes that she has fallen (ibid., 62). The narrator emphasizes that Montraville "robbed" Charlotte of her innocence (ibid., 66). This carefully constructed scene indicts Montraville as a seducer who uses pressure and coercion to manipulate Charlotte; this scene represents the epitome of acquaintance rape.

At certain junctures, Montraville does express some personal responsibility for misleading Charlotte, but only after her death. At this point, Montraville expresses his realization that he deliberately led a fifteen-year-old astray through deception, manipulation, and coercion. "I am a seducer, a mean, ungenerous seducer of unsuspecting innocence," exclaims Montraville in a moment of dejection (ibid., 87, 93). Montraville further recognizes that he failed to consider the consequences of his actions, especially when he had been forewarned by his father not to gratify his passions by leading young girls away from the security of their homes (ibid., 38).

Of course, *Female Quixotism* also illustrates quite graphically the tragedy a woman can encounter when she ventures forth from the security of her home. Throughout *Female Quixotism*, the heroine participates in a series of adventures in which she is the object of seduction. Because she is a privileged woman with an extensive inheritance, Dorcasina Sheldon is the prey of scheming profligates. In one seduction, the rake Patrick O'Connor is described as the prototypical fortune-hunter who views his prospective relationship with Dorcasina in essentially oppositional terms: "As for O'Connor, he went strutting to his lodgings, felicitating himself upon his invention and address, and laying plans for the management of [Dorcasina's] fair domain, of which he had not the least doubt of soon gaining possession" (Tenney [1801] 1992, 29). O'Connor is not the only fortune-hunter to traverse the pages of *Female*

Quixotism; there are many other seducers and abusers who act either alone or in the company of other schemers. Clearly, the violence levied against Dorcasina and her maid reveals the presence of a rape culture during the eighteenth century.

Often, women have been taught through fear that to venture forth into the night unescorted could endanger their lives; and, of course, Dorcasina experiences just this. After she travels to a local inn with O'Connor, Dorcasina discovers that he is a fortune-hunter and thus rejects him as a prospective husband. Because he has been found out, O'Connor decides to seek revenge against Dorcasina. When he sees a gang of boys outside the inn, O'Connor falsely warns them that Dorcasina is a disguised hooligan who has come to raise havoc. At this point, the narrator compares Dorcasina to a "poor timid hare" who has been beset by "hunters" (ibid., 60). After Dorcasina frees herself from O'Connor, she sets out for her home. Suddenly, she is overcome by the rowdy boys who are "hallowing, and endeavoring with all their might to overtake her" (ibid.). Exhausted from trying to escape them, Dorcasina is overtaken by the pack. At this point, the boys "strip" off parts of her clothing—her gown, bonnet, and handkerchief—and leave her with only some "tattered remains" (ibid.). After much struggling, Dorcasina frees herself from her assailants and runs for safety. While *Female Quixotism* does contain warnings and injunctions to women about the dangers that lurk outside the domestic realm, it also points to the existence of a rape culture that fosters rape, assault, sexual harassment, and physical and verbal abuse—the most tragic methods of maintaining women's compliance to gender roles and social expectations.

In *Stopping Rape*, Rus Funk explores violence against women as both personal and political crimes (1993, 27). Like Stoltenberg, Funk deconstructs masculinity and exposes the elements of culture that support violence against women and rape as "expression[s] of male privilege" (ibid., 34). Funk reminds his audience that men rape for a variety of reasons, including their desires for power, control, and dominance—all encouraged and fostered by patriarchy, a systematic, naturalized form of male supremacy (ibid., 29,34). As noted by Brownmiller and Funk, rape or seduction becomes a form of sexual politics—a form of social control that keeps women in their prescribed place through fear, intimidation, and the threat of male sexual aggression and violence. Most poignantly, Nancy Biele and Peggy Miller in "Twenty Years Later" conclude that rape represents the ultimate perversion of patriarchal power (1993, 49).

If a woman dares to transgress her patriarchally prescribed role and identity, she is seen as inviting danger, rape, and sexual harassment, as in the cases of Charlotte Temple, Mary Lumley, Eliza Wharton, and Dorcasina Sheldon. Rape, then and now, epitomizes the ultimate reenactment of the relationship between the colonized and the colonizer. As a colonizer, a rapist can forcibly violate a woman's body as a reaffirmation of his power just as he can depend upon a woman's fear and shame to keep this act a secret. Today, as well as during the eighteenth century, a woman is often blamed for a man's sexual transgression, just as Eve is blamed for Adam's decision to transgress God's law, and just as Eve's descendants—Charlotte Temple, Eliza Wharton and Dorcasina Sheldon—are blamed for overstepping their prescribed lots.

What, then, are the effects of seduction upon women? Although many contemporary theorists are doing groundbreaking multidisciplinary studies of seduction and rape, Foster, Tenney, Murray, and Rowson well documented the consequences of seduction and the stereotype of the fallen woman on the female mind, body, and spirit two hundred years ago. In "I Just Raped My Wife," Carol Adams notes that rape violates a person's spirit and body (1993, 72). Indeed, the novels under evaluation portray seduction and rape as more than crimes against fathers; they, in fact, represent seduction as a crime against the woman herself. As Adams notes, the perpetuation of this violence depends upon women keeping silent about the guilt, shame, contamination, degradation, defilement, and powerlessness they often feel as a result of being denied the right to control their own bodies (ibid.). These feelings, though, are not unique to the twentieth-century woman or contemporary novelists such as Alice Walker, Toni Morrison, Amy Tan, and Louise Erdrich who write about rape and rape culture. These same feelings and long-term consequences of rape and seduction are experienced by Mary Lumley, Dorcasina Sheldon, Charlotte Temple, and Eliza Wharton—the most memorable characters in late eighteenth-century American seduction narratives. In the book, In *Other Worlds: Essays in Cultural Politics*, Spivak argues that often the colonized or "subaltern" women are silenced, in part, because they have no space from which to speak

(1987, 122). While the socio-political milieu of the late eighteenth century certainly fosters the silencing of women of different races and classes, the eighteenth-century novel of seduction provides a forum for some fallen women to disclose their silent lives of desperation. Although the eighteenth-century seduction novel may be considered a work of fiction, it is at a fundamental level a tale of truth embedded in realities that were often concealed from the public realm, perhaps because of its indifference.

Among the narratives in question, *The Coquette* provides the most comprehensive development of the physical and psychological decline of a woman who becomes the prey of a profligate. The intensity of Eliza's decline is further emphasized by the dramatic transformation she undergoes. In the beginning of the novel, Eliza's joyous internal world reflects her optimistic external environment. As she becomes deeply entwined in the marriage crisis, Eliza's internal world becomes afflicted and disordered as does her external environment (Foster [1797] 1986, 89).

Eliza's physical and psychological decline is primarily triggered by Boyer's stereotyping of her as a fallen woman. Although Eliza reluctantly consents to an engagement with Boyer, Boyer breaks the engagement after he interrupts a clandestine meeting between Eliza and Sanford. Although he condemns Eliza for meeting with Sanford, Boyer does not realize that Sanford initiated the contact in hopes of pressuring her to break her engagement. As a result of Boyer's rash reduction of her to a coquette, Eliza is devastated. Because this hostile encounter with Boyer has caused her "the most painful anxiety" of mind, Eliza realizes that she is forever altered. In an allusion to *Macbeth*, Eliza comes to the tragic recognition that sleep will no longer provide a balm for her hurt mind (ibid., 93). At this point, Eliza has lost only one legitimate suitor, but there appear to be no other suitors for the thirty-seven-year-old woman.

Faced with the harsh realization of her economically bleak future, Eliza attempts to initiate a reconciliation with Boyer and, perhaps, even a reunion with him. Boyer, though, meets Eliza with further disdain. His continued denunciation of her spurs Eliza to regret apologizing to him; she exclaims: "Oh that I had not written to Mr. Boyer! by confessing my faults, and by avowing my partiality to him, I have given him the power of triumphing in my distress" (ibid., 105). As an astute and perceptive individual, Eliza realizes that she has been in a power struggle with Boyer. In her assessment of her situation, she realizes still further that she relinquished her power to him by admitting that she should have terminated her association with Sanford. Eliza's powerlessness devastates her particularly because she also relinquishes her quest for independence. With a sullied reputation and no financial security, Eliza confronts a desolate future in the new republic; there is no respectable space for a fallen woman to occupy.

Humiliated by the turn of events, Eliza internalizes the guilt others think she should feel. Even if she begged forgiveness from her friends and family, Eliza realizes that "the dye is absolutely cast" (ibid., 94). The stereotype of the fallen woman and the opinions of others determine Eliza's future course. When she succumbs to the opinion of others, Eliza is also forced to reassess her life and sadly conclude: "The events of my life have always been unaccountably wayward. In many instances, I have been ready to suppose that some evil genius presided over my actions, which has directed them contrary to the sober dictates of my own judgment" (ibid., 108). Rather tragically, Eliza internalizes the fatalistic or predeterministic perspective she so desired to cast off. Consequently, Eliza lapses into a state of depression.

Withdrawn and despondent, Eliza becomes "locked in the body"— the site where the symptoms of her despair manifest themselves (ibid., 91, 94). Through her deteriorating body, family and friends read Eliza's despair. In a letter to his friend, Sanford explains the striking transformation that Eliza has undergone since their first meeting: "Eliza is extremely altered! Her pale dejected countenance, with the sedateness of her manners, so different from the lively glow of health, cheerfulness and activity which formerly animated her appearance and deportment, struck me very disagreeably" (ibid., 125). Despite Eliza's intense suffering, Sanford is not deterred from seducing her into a temporary sexual relationship. Rather than relinquish his plans, Sanford chooses to use his resourcefulness and prey upon Eliza's vulnerability. A friend of the Wharton family, Julia Granby, fears that Eliza has no strength or "resolution to resist temptation" from Sanford (ibid., 131). While Sanford focuses upon the physical alteration of Eliza, Julia focuses upon Eliza's emotional and psychological deterioration, particularly when she concludes that Eliza's mind is "surprisingly weakened" (ibid.). Although family and friends recognize Eliza's suffering, they are hesitant to broach the subject with her because they realize that she attempts to conceal her "symptoms" from them. Family and friends are uncertain if Eliza's illness is "any real disorder of the body, or whether it arose from her depression of spirits" (ibid., 138). Alert to the intricate connection between the mind and the body, Eliza feels that the physical and the emotional symptoms "operated together" to produce the decline in her health (ibid.). Eliza even admits that she now fears her "own reflections, which ought to be a constant source of enjoyment" (ibid., 115). She admits further that she can no longer bear lengthy letter writing, a once pleasurable endeavor (ibid., 127). As the novel reaches its dramatic conclusion, Eliza grows increasingly silent and dejected.

Eliza's suffering over her fallen status is not unique to her; other fallen heroines in the novels of Rowson, Tenney, and Murray suffer as well. Like Eliza, Charlotte Temple suffers physically and emotionally from her tragedy. As the narrative progresses and her situation becomes more desperate, Charlotte's physical and psychological illnesses intensify. As she grows more pale and emaciated, Charlotte experiences fits of faintness. Just before her death, Charlotte's appearance alters so drastically that friends barely recognize her (Rowson [1794] 1986, 112). While Montraville participates in "lawless pleasure," Charlotte sinks "unnoticed to the grave, a prey to sickness, grief, and penury" (ibid., 98). As the novel progresses to its conventional conclusion, Charlotte succumbs to "a violent depression" (ibid., 101). By the time she gives birth, she is already on the brink of death. Perhaps because she cannot bear the burden of her plight, Charlotte begins to disassociate herself from her condition by referring to herself in the third person. The narrator emphasizes that Charlotte's delirium was so intense that she was unaware of the fact that she was a mother (ibid., 112). In *Lucy Temple*, Mary Lumley also suffers from postpartum delirium (Rowson [1828] 1991, 252). "Thin and wasted," Mary Lumley suffers from a fever that deprives her of her "reason" (ibid.). Mary, though, survives her illness and is welcomed back into the Matthews family (ibid., 255). Charlotte Temple, however, does not recover from her fever.

Eliza Wharton also does not recuperate from the physical and emotional distress subsequent to her seduction. The details of the seduction and the emotional consequences, though, are not narrated by Eliza herself but rather by Julia Granby. In a letter to a friend, Julia Granby explains the events that transpired the day she discovered Eliza's affair with Sanford. When Julia confronts Eliza about her evening encounters with Sanford in Mrs. Wharton's parlor, Eliza admits that Sanford "robbed" her of her peace and "triumphed" in her ruin (Foster [1797] 1986, 142). Untouched by Eliza's story, Julia harshly reprimands her friend and hopes that she will be able to bear her "infamy." Eliza recognizes that she will have to bear the horror of this situation, but she does ask Julia to pity her decaying frame. Because she feels that her body can no longer sustain existence, Eliza asks friends and family for mercy and compassion. Instead, Julia Granby further condemns Eliza because she feels that Eliza recognized Sanford as a Lovelace (ibid., 143). Devastated by the harsh criticisms of others, Eliza realizes that she cannot alter past events. Perhaps the only way she can exert any amount of control over her situation is by refusing her already ailing body food. Consequently, she grows more emaciated as the novel reaches its conclusion. The physical and psychological disorders that afflict Eliza become her only hope for redemption. As the Puritan script often dictates, Eliza suffers for her transgressive act; however, Eliza's suffering is not spurred primarily by her "sin" but rather by society's rejection and condemnation of her.

Although she recognizes Sanford as a seducer, Eliza admits that she could not resist him. Why, then, does this astute and intelligent woman succumb to a man she perceives as a rake? In a letter to a friend, Julia Granby discloses the reasons Eliza offers for her submission to Sanford. In this secondhand account, Eliza admits that Sanford offered her consolation when her friends and family could not. Although friends and family recognize Eliza's suffering, they are hesitant to confront her on the cause. Rather than contribute further to the intensity of her decline, family and friends try to occupy Eliza's time with amusements (ibid., 110). Diversions, though, could not console Eliza's suffering. Thus, she turns to Sanford. Eliza admits that she would have fled from Sanford if she could, but her "circumstances called for attention" (ibid., 146). Further, Eliza admits:

I had no one to participate my cares, to witness my distress, and to alleviate my sorrows, but [Sanford]. I could not therefore prevail on myself, wholly to renounce his society. At times I have admitted his visits; always meeting him in the garden, . . . and my ill health induced me to comply with his solicitations, and receive him into the parlor (ibid., 145–46).

Although she recognizes him as a profligate, Eliza feels that Sanford is a source of comfort. But because he is married, Sanford's affair with Eliza is even more scandalous. Although he has no intention of developing a long-term relationship with her, Sanford strategically slithers into Eliza's favor in order to seduce her. Indeed, Sanford demonstrates a shrewd and perceptive strategy in his seduction of Eliza because he not only understands her vulnerability, but he also actively chooses to prey upon it in order to achieve his long-awaited victory.

Interestingly, when Eliza writes her last letter to her mother verifying her fallen status, she, like Charlotte Temple, refers to herself with a detached otherness. In her final letter to her mother, Eliza professes: " . . . your Eliza has fallen; fallen. . . . She has become the victim of her own indiscretion, and of the intrigue and artifice of a designing libertine. . . . She is polluted, and no more worthy of her parentage. She flies from you . . . " (ibid., 153). Overwhelmed with guilt and the feelings shared by other victims of rape, Eliza attempts to disassociate herself from her victimization by referring to herself in the third person. Although she perceives her actions as criminal, she believes that her crime is primarily against her family rather than herself (ibid., 154).

Whether consciously or unconsciously, Eliza understands the Connecticut and Massachusetts laws that define a woman who engages in premarital sex with a married man as an adulterer. In Puritan New England, men and women who committed fornication could face the death penalty, branding, lashing, imprisonment, and even the infamous scarlet letter (Benson 1935, 226). Even if they endured their severe punishments, fallen women still were considered prostitutes who transgressed not only societal law but God's law (Koehler 1980, 148). By the late eighteenth century, the enforcing of fornication laws regarding women waned. In fact, by 1800 Connecticut and Massachusetts stopped indicting women for fornication (Shuffelton 1986, 214). This is not to suggest that fornication laws regarding women ceased to exist. In 1785, Massachusetts altered its fornication laws by punishing offenders primarily with fines (Benson 1935, 227). Given the political milieu of the late eighteenth century, Charlotte Temple, Mary Lumley, and Eliza Wharton certainly would not have been punished legally for fornication, but neither would their seducers. When Sanford, Courtland, and O'Connor are penalized by the law, they are punished for crimes—theft and bankruptcy—other than fornication or rape.

In "To Ravish and Carnally Know," Barbara Lindemann offers some insight into the reasons motivating eighteenth-century Massachusetts for not recognizing seduction as rape. If a woman was an acquaintance of her alleged rapist, she would have to go to great lengths to convince an all-male jury that she did not give consent (Lindemann 1984, 68). Since Eliza Wharton willingly placed herself in the company of Sanford, regardless of the fact that he systematically set out to mislead and conquer her, she is viewed as giving consent. In addition, religious zealots believed that a woman would not have been able to bear a child if she was raped. According to Puritan theology, God would never allow a child to be brought forth under such heinous circumstances (ibid., 67). Of course, Mary Lumley, Charlotte Temple, and Eliza Wharton all bear children. In some instances, a woman's word would not be enough to convict an alleged rapist. Additional factors such as physical bruises and witnesses were necessary to convict an individual of rape unless special circumstances were presented like the rape of a minor. Issues of race and class also factored into convictions or acquittals. For instance, if a slave woman accused her owner of rape, her accusation would be dismissed because she was legally the slave- owner's property, and he was merely exercising his property rights. "To ravage and carnally know"—a standard legal definition of rape—was quite difficult to prove. If a woman accused a man of rape, she would have to exert a tremendous amount of strength before family, friends, and an all-male jury, for she was still considered damaged goods, and her worth on the marriage market would be severely diminished (ibid., 65). During the seventeenth century, Puritan minister John Cotton preached that, regardless of whether a woman engaged freely in premarital sex or was raped, she was a fallen woman. During the eighteenth century, this belief was still embraced by many (Koehler 1980, 74).

As a fallen woman with no legal recourse, Eliza Wharton can find solace only through penance and forgiveness from her mother: "The only hope which affords me any solace, is that of your forgiveness. If the deepest contrition can make an atonement; if the severest pains, both of body and mind, can restore me to your charity, you will not be inexorable!" (Foster [1797] 1986, 154). Not only does Eliza embrace her severe suffering, but she embraces it with the hope that she will be purged of her sin (ibid., 155).

In the end, Eliza has been seduced not only by Sanford but also by her friends and family into believing that her desire to live a life dictated by the Declaration of Independence was ridiculous. In "Domesticating Virtue," Carroll Smith-Rosenberg observes that Eliza's fall to Sanford is secondary. Eliza's primary fall is "to the authoritative male discourse of her age. She has relinquished her quest to fuse independence and pleasure . . . " (Smith-Rosenberg 1988, 177). Because of intense societal pressure and ridicule, Eliza succumbs to her culture's notion of "true womanhood."

After their seductions and subsequent pregnancies, Eliza Wharton and Charlotte Temple hope that death will claim them quickly. At one point, Charlotte Temple even contemplates suicide, but because she is a Christian and suicide is a sin against God, she eventually rejects the idea. This illustrates, though, the extent of Charlotte's desperation. Instead of directly committing suicide, she wishes for death to claim her because only in death will she be at peace (Rowson [1794] 1986, 74). Because she, too, has "not a single wish to live" (Foster [1797] 1986, 146), Eliza wills herself to die. Her emaciated frame attests to her desire to restrict her eating and succumb to death. Distraught and emaciated, Charlotte Temple and Eliza Wharton both die of puerperal fever.

In *Fasting Girls: The History of Anorexia Nervosa*, Joan Brumberg explores some of the conditions that have historically compelled women to use appetite as a form of self-expression and communication (1989, 3). Fallen heroines such as Charlotte Temple, Mary Lumley, Dorcasina Sheldon, and Eliza Wharton do not necessarily suffer from anorexia nervosa, however, several explanations offered by Brumberg about women's food restriction provide insight into the deteriorating lives of these fallen heroines. During the medieval age, religious women often used food restriction to "express religious ideals of suffering and service to their fellow creatures" (ibid., 45). If she suppressed her appetite, a religious woman symbolized piety and submission (ibid.). While Eliza Wharton, Charlotte Temple, and Mary Lumley are not the products of medieval Europe, they are the products of Puritan and Christian heritages that recognize suffering as an essential component of life on earth. Because Eliza, Mary, and Charlotte endure profound anguish subsequent to their falls, they are viewed by friends and family as penitent. From a societal perspective, suffering becomes the only viable means for a fallen woman to redeem herself.

The religious imagery and sermonic tone that pervade *Charlotte Temple* help portray the fallen heroine as a religious figure. In *Love and Death in the American Novel*, Leslie Fiedler acknowledges that Charlotte is portrayed as a martyr. Although he views *Charlotte Temple* as a "banal form" of a Richardsonian story, Fiedler argues that Rowson "succeeded in projecting once and for all the American woman's image of herself as the long-suffering martyr of love—the inevitable victim of male brutality and lust" (1992, 97). Indeed, Charlotte is both a victim and a martyr. She is the prey of a seducer who possesses a rapist ethic and is a sufferer, not because of "love," but because cultural traditions have made her feel that she committed a great atrocity.

The story itself portrays Charlotte as a sacrificial victim. Just before her death, the abandoned Charlotte seeks out her former teacher, La Rue, for assistance. Because she does not want the burden of a destitute and pregnant Charlotte, La Rue, like the Apostle Peter, denies three times that she knows Charlotte (Rowson [1794] 1986, 108). Because they sympathize with her tragedy, servants take the penniless Charlotte into their meager "hovel" until her death. In this impoverished setting, Mr. Temple reunites with his daughter. Repossessed by her father and forgiven for her tragedy, Charlotte experiences a final moment of happiness as "a sudden beam of joy passed across her languid features" (ibid., 116). In a scene reminiscent of religious icons and paintings, Charlotte raises her "eyes to heaven" and expires (ibid.). With the surname of Temple, Charlotte, regardless of her seduction, remains a sacred being. Like many of Rowson's protagonists, claims Dorothy Weil, Charlotte projects a Christ-like image (1976, 72).

The religious undertones that pervade the narratives of seduction by Rowson, Foster, Murray, and Tenney are not the only possible aids to the interpretation of the physical and psychological suffering of fallen heroines. Brumberg argues that, when young women have no emotional outlet, they often direct their anger, fear, and despair toward themselves through the control of their appetite (1989, 138). In *Starving in the Silences*, Martra Robertson observes that often the body a woman denies food is not only the physical body that may be suffering from illness but also a body that is a both a symbolic and cultural "product of an ideology" (1992, 64). When heroines refuse food, they surrender to death. Albeit indirectly, when a woman denies herself food, she is committing suicide.

Since there is no respectable cultural space for a fallen woman to inhabit, death becomes the only alternative.

All the fallen heroines encountered in the seduction narratives under review long, at some point, for death to claim their forsaken lives. Denying themselves food becomes the only method for some women, according to Robertson, "to express themselves within a dominant gender order where women's power is unequal to men's" (1992, xiii). Because all the fallen heroines are described, at some point, as emaciated, depressed, and desirous of death, their suffering becomes an essential component of the seduction paradigm. When her voice is silenced or usurped, a heroine communicates her suffering through pain and sorrow.

When Michel Foucault asks "What difference does it make who is speaking?" he fails to consider that the person doing the speaking often already has a privileged space as a subject (1977, 138). For the fallen heroine with neither a legally recognized voice nor a legally recognized subjectivity, speaking symbolizes political identity. Had Charlotte Temple and Mary Lumley not been usurped of their power to speak and to communicate through letters, they could have procured help from friends and relatives. In "Charlotte Temple and the End of Epistolarity," Blythe Forcey also observes that Charlotte cannot communicate her will effectively because she was not taught effective communication skills. Forcey argues that, because Charlotte was trained to be trusting and obedient to authority, she could neither speak nor understand the language of her new life in a new world (1991, 237). Yet, for Charlotte, speaking could have meant the difference between life and death.

Since an eighteenth-century woman by law had no recognizable voice, how could she deny the patriarchy its privileged access to her body? Thus, the coquette and the fallen woman are stereotypes created to describe transgressive women; but they are also labels that shift the blame from patriarchy onto women. As property, the daughter and wife are possessed by the father and husband. If a young woman leaves her paternal roof, she is legally dispossessed; she belongs to neither father nor husband. When she leaves her home for Massachusetts, Eliza is the epitome of the dispossessed woman. For many conservatives, Eliza Wharton, Mary Lumley, and Charlotte Temple represent familial and societal disruption—everything the new republic did not want. However, with such novels as *The Coquette, Female Quixotism, Charlotte Temple,*

and *Lucy Temple* representing the existence of a rape culture and exposing seducers as criminals, the stereotypes of the coquette and the fallen
woman are disrupted. For, after all, these novels allow female characters
to call directly for the branding and the eradication of male seducers
from society. . . nay from the earth. In *The Coquette*, Lucy Freeman fearlessly offers her perspective on the fatal effects of seducers. Lucy
believes that the "vicious" Sanford is far worse than "the robber and the
assassin" because when the latter criminals are detected they are punished by law. Boldly, Lucy Freeman compares a seducer to

> an assassin of honor; the wretch, who breaks the peace of fami-
> lies, who robs virgin innocence of its charms, who triumphs over
> the ill placed confidence of the inexperienced, unsuspecting,
> and too credulous fair, is received, and caressed, not only by his
> own sex, to which he is a reproach, but even by ours, who have
> every conceivable reason to despise and avoid him. (Foster
> [1797] 1986, 65)

Clearly, Lucy Freeman conveys her understanding that a young woman's
reputation is equated with her chastity. Conscious of this perspective,
Sanford also equates a woman's honor with her "chastity" (ibid., 125). If
this chastity does not remain intact, a woman's worth on the marriage
market and in society is depleted. The narratives under consideration
emphasize that often a woman's worth is determined by society. If society deems a woman unfeminine, rebellious, and disrespectful, then she
is labeled a fallen woman. As consciousness-raising texts, the narratives
call for the re-evaluation of fallen women, seducers, and rapists.
According to Lucy Freeman, seducers must be branded as criminals who
should be punished for their actions. Even more boldly than Lucy
Freeman, the narrator of *Charlotte Temple* admits that she wishes she
had the "power to extirpate those monsters of seduction from the earth"
(Rowson [1794] 1986, 29).

As didactic texts, many seduction narratives forewarn the American
fair and American society itself about the fatal effects of seducers. In *The
Coquette*, Eliza hopes that her "unhappy story [will] serve as a beacon
to warn the American fair of the dangerous tendency and destructive
consequences of associating with men" like Sanford (Foster [1797]

1986, 159). She hopes that the "deluded creatures" of the world will rise up against the rakes and seducers in judgment and condemnation (ibid.). Similarly, Charlotte Temple hopes that her tale will be retold (Rowson [1794] 1986, 81). Charlotte's plea for the re-telling of her tragic story is part of Rowson's greater call for the re-education of the American fair. Patricia Parker argues that Rowson wanted young women to transform their fundamental way of viewing the world; they needed to think "about the world in an unromantic . . . way" (1986, 47).

The narrative strategy of storytelling incorporated into many senti-mental novels can be both instructive and cathartic. According to Clarissa Estes, storytelling has the potential to act as both a balm to heal hurt minds and a form of instruction that guides the development of the listener's psyche as it passes on vital information about life (1992, 15). The narratives of seduction by Rowson, Foster, Tenney, and Murray often impart to their readers vital instruction that they will need to approach the next phase of their lives, not only in a new nation, but in a new century.

In *Stopping Rape: A Challenge for Men*, Funk observes that, when women live in fear of violence and rape, they cannot live freely (1993, 14). In *Transforming A Rape Culture*, the editors argue that in order for women to live lives of freedom—freedom from being sexual prey—the world must change. In their call for social transformation, Roth, Fletcher, and Buchwald ask their readers to participate in a new vision: "We must imagine a different world. If we can dream of a safe place, surely we can build one. . . . we challenge our readers to help us make these changes. Please join us in envisioning and building a humane future" (1993, 3). On some level, the novels under review share this vision, for in order to build a humane future for women, society must first recognize the existence of violence against women. The novels of Rowson, Foster, Tenney, and Murray not only point to the existence of a rape culture, but they also actively educate their audience about ways to transform it.

Conclusion:
A New Era of Female History

A̲ltho̲ugh̲ t̲he̲ t̲heme̲ of seduction provided the staple of many early American novels, it was more than formulaic fiction that traced the fall of a heroine. It was a theme tightly woven into the fabric of the early nation. The seduction narratives of Murray, Tenney, Foster, and Rowson reflect not only the concerns of a new nation experimenting with a new government, but also the concerns of a particular segment of the population—young middle- and upper-class women—seduced by the hope offered by the War for Independence and later abandoned when they claimed and were denied the rights to life, liberty, and the pursuit of happiness as their own.

The unalienable rights that the patriots arduously embraced raised significant questions with significant ramifications. If all men were created equal, did all men have a voice in government and in the direction of the new nation? Of course, women of all races and classes were deliberately absent from this declaration of equality. Since they were excluded from the sentiments of the Declaration of Independence, did women, then, have the right to rebel and institute a new government that would recognize their unalienable rights? Indeed, John Adams expressed his concerns over these significant consequences in his apt and intriguing declaration that "Democracy is Lovelace and the people are Clarissa" (Fliegelman 1982, 237). Adams feared that the spirit of democracy that permeated America would cause men and women to be ruled by unrestrained passion rather than human reason and human consciousness (ibid., 237). For Adams and his colleagues, only a select few had the capacity to reason—white, male property owners over the age of eighteen. If power was not restrained with reason and balance from the masses, America, John Adams feared, would embrace the fate of Clarissa. The young nation, too, would be seduced and abandoned.

107

In the novels under review, the "American fair" is seduced and abandoned. Perhaps the fear that young women would embrace the fate of Clarissa motivated these New England authors to cast their novels as forewarnings with didactic agendas. Young women needed to understand that, although they longed to embrace their declarations of independence, they were systematically denied this right by the nation's founding fathers. Fostered and perpetuated by a variety of conditions in the early nation, seduction represents the politically charged practice of neocolonialism.

The narratives of seduction under consideration offer social critiques of a nation that—rather than blame the social environment that fostered the fall of many women—blamed women themselves for men's transgressions. Thus, the seductions of Charlotte Temple, Frances Wellwood, Eliza Wharton, Dorcasina Sheldon, Mary Lumley, and their counterparts represent a complex signifying practice determined and reproduced by limited educational opportunities, colonial laws and customs, circumscribed roles for the middle-class woman, and the existence of a rape culture. While many narratives of seduction may be read as allegories of woman's sin in transgressing her prescribed role and her punishment in dying shortly after delivering the product of her transgression, these readings cannot be fully sustained in the novels under consideration, for they portray woman's fall as a consequence of a much greater social problem—man's imperialist desire to subdue and conquer.

The writings of Murray, Tenney, Foster, and Rowson contribute to a call for the decolonization of women. In "Foucault on Power: A Theory for Women?" Hartsock discusses some of the necessary steps women need to take in the decolonization of their status: "The critical steps are, first, using what we know about our lives as a basis for critique of the dominant culture and, second, creating alternatives" (1990, 172). Indeed, these four authors do not critique their world without offering alternative perspectives and courses of action to transform society and the lot of women. While seduction narratives have been labeled novels of victimization, the novels of these four writers depict, not only who is doing the victimizing and why, but what is at stake for the new nation if the lives of women are not freed from this systematic and calculated oppression. Coupled with feminist theory and cultural studies, postcolonial theory offers another means of re-examining seduction narratives created in an era in which the foundation of contemporary society was created.

During the nineteenth century, the roles of women in society expanded further as did their roles in literature. However, the themes explored in eighteenth-century novels of seduction do not entirely disappear; they are re-explored and re-invented in many nineteenth-century novels. Most appropriately, Walter Wenska argues that "the distance between seventeenth-century Boston and late eighteenth-century New Haven is not great. Nor is it much farther to mid-nineteenth-century Concord or New York" (1977–78, 253). Central to the eighteenth-century novel, the themes of seduction and the fallen woman are still being examined in the writings of Nathaniel Hawthorne, Louisa May Alcott, Susan Warner, and Edith Wharton.

The themes explored in the writings of Murray, Tenney, Foster, and Rowson did not touch only the literary world of the nineteenth century. In particular, the critiques of the *Feme Sole* and the *Feme Covert* offered in seduction narratives found further illustration in the writings, speeches, and actions of many nineteenth-century feminists. In addition to their mission to end slavery, Angelina and Sarah Grimké, two Quaker sisters, also educated the public on women's rights. In "Letters on the Equality of the Sexes and the Condition of Women," Sarah Grimké addresses many of the same issues addressed by Murray in "On the Equality of the Sexes" in 1790. Similarly, Margaret Fuller in *Woman in the Nineteenth Century* dispels the myths that women are inferior to men and calls for the expansion of women's rights, including the rights to vote and preach. At the first organized women's rights convention at Seneca Falls, New York, in 1848, Elizabeth Cady Stanton, Susan B. Anthony, and others argued for changes in women's property laws and for women's right to vote. As it resonated with the republican rhetoric of the late eighteenth century, Stanton's *Declaration of Sentiments* reminded America that women, too, deserved to possess the unalienable rights to life, liberty, and the pursuit of happiness.

Often the nineteenth century is associated with the emergence of the nation's first organized women's movement; but, in actuality, pioneers in women's rights can be traced to the late eighteenth century. Indeed, the consciousness-raising seduction narratives under review not only re-educate the American fair about their condition in the new republic but also forewarn them about the dangers of their disenfranchised status. In *Stopping Rape*, Rus Funk argues that "Education is an invaluable tool for creating change. Education is a process of learning new skills and new ways of looking at the world" (1993, 117). The narratives of seduction by Murray, Rowson, Foster, and Tenney encourage their young middle- and upper-class readers to learn new skills and alternative ways of viewing their world. With these new tools, young readers can contribute individually to a social and political transformation of a mass consciousness. "I may be accused of enthusiasm," contends Murray in "Observations on Female Abilities," "but such is my confidence in the female sex, that I expect to see our young women forming a new era in female history" ([1797] 1992, 703).

Works Cited

Adams, Abigail, and John Adams. "'Remember the Ladies': Abigail Adams v. John Adams." In *The Feminist Papers: From Adams to de Beauvoir*, ed. Alice S. Rossi, 7–15. Boston: Northeastern University Press, 1988.

Adams, Carol. "'I Just Raped My Wife! What Are You Going To Do About It, Pastor?': The Church and Sexual Violence." In *Transforming A Rape Culture*, ed. by Emilie Buchwald, Pamela Fletcher, and Martha Roth, 57–86. Minneapolis, Minn.: Milkweed, 1993.

Ashcroft, Bill, Gareth Griffiths, and Helen Tiffin. *The Empire Writes Back*. New York: Routledge, 1989.

Baym, Nina. *Woman's Fiction: A Guide to Novels by and about Women in America, 1820–1870*. Ithaca, NY: Cornell University Press, 1978.

———. Introduction to *The Gleaner*, by Judith Sargent Murray, iii–xx. Schenectady, NY: Union College Press, 1992.

Benson, Mary Sumner. *Women in Eighteenth-Century America: A Study of Opinion and Social Usage*. Port Washington, NY: Kennikat Press, 1935.

Biele, Nancy, and Peggy Miller. "Twenty Years Later: The Unfinished Revolution." In *Transforming A Rape Culture*, ed. by Emilie Buchwald, Pamela Fletcher, and Martha Roth, 47–56. Minneapolis, Minn.: Milkweed, 1993.

Bolton, Charles. *The Elizabeth Whitman Mystery*. Peabody, Mass.: Peabody Historical Society, 1912.

Bradstreet, Anne. "The Prologue." In vol. 1 of *The Norton Anthology of American Literature*, 4th ed. by Nina Baym et al., 200. New York: Norton and Company, 1994.

Brown, Herbert Ross. *The Sentimental Novel in America, 1789–1860*. Freeport, NY: Books for Libraries Press, 1940.

Brown, William Hill. *The Power of Sympathy*. Columbus: Ohio State University Press, 1969.

Brownmiller, Susan. *Against Our Will: Men, Women and Rape*. New York: Fawcett Columbine, 1975.

Brumberg, Joan Jacobs. *Fasting Girls: The History of Anorexia Nervosa*. New York: Penguin Books, 1989.

Buchwald, Emilie, Pamela Fletcher, and Martha Roth, eds. *Transforming A Rape Culture*. Minneapolis, Minn.: Milkweed Editions, 1993.

Chambers-Schiller, Lee Virginia. *Liberty, A Better Husband: Single Women in America, The Generations of 1780–1840*. New Haven, Conn.: Yale University Press, 1984.

Collins, Andrea and Jean Nienkamp, eds. Introduction to *Female Quixotism*, xiii–xxvi. New York: Oxford University Press, 1992.

Cott, Nancy. *The Bonds of Womanhood: Woman's Sphere in New England, 1780–1835*. New Haven, Conn.: Yale University Press, 1977.

Dall, C. W. H. *The Romance of Association: or, One Last Glimpse of Charlotte Temple and Eliza Wharton, A Curiosity of Literature and Life*. Cambridge, Mass.: John Wilson & Son, 1875.

Davidson, Cathy. "Hannah Webster Foster." In Vol. 37 of *Dictionary of Literary Biography: American Writers of the Early Republic*, ed. by Emory Elliot, 161–63. Detroit: Book Tower, 1985.

——— ed. Introduction to *The Coquette*, vii–xx. New York: Oxford University Press, 1986.

———. *Revolution and The Word: The Rise of the American Novel*. New York: Oxford University Press, 1986.

Davis, Angela. *Women, Race, and Class*. New York: Vintage Books, 1983.

Douglas. Ann. Introduction to *Charlotte Temple and Lucy Temple*, vii–xliii. Boston: Penguin Books, 1991.

During, Simon. "Postmodernism or Postcolonialism Today." In *The Post-Colonial Studies Reader*, ed. by Bill Ashcroft, Gareth Griffiths, and Helen Tiffin, 125–29. New York: Routledge, 1995.

Ebert, Teresa L. "The Difference of Postmodern Feminism." *College English* 53 (1991): 886–904.

Estes, Clarissa Pinkola. *Women Who Run With the Wolves*. New York: Ballantine, 1992.

Evans, Sara. *Born For Liberty*. New York: Free Press, 1989.

Evans, Martha Noel. "Hysteria and the Seduction of Theory." In *Seduction and Theory: Readings of Gender, Representation and Rhetoric*, ed. by Dianne Hunter, 73–85. Urbana: University of Illinois Press, 1989.

Field, Vena Bernadette. *Constantia: A Study of the Life & Works of Judith Sargent Murray*. Orono: Maine University Press, 1931.

Fiedler, Leslie. *Love and Death in the American Novel*. New York: Anchor Books, 1992.

Fisher, Marguerite. "Eighteenth-Century Theorists of Women's Liberation." In *"Remember the Ladies": New Perspectives on Women in American History*, ed. by Carol George, 39–47. Syracuse, NY: Syracuse University Press, 1975.

Fizer, Irene. "Signing As Republican Daughters: The Letters of Eliza Southgate and *The Coquette*." *The Eighteenth Century* 34, no. 3 (1993): 243–63.

Fliegelman, Jay. *Prodigals and Pilgrims: The American Revolution Against Patriarchal Authority*. New York: Cambridge University Press, 1982.

Forcey, Blythe. "Charlotte Temple and the End of Epistolarity." *American Literature* 63 (1991): 225–41.

Foster, Hannah. *The Boarding School*. Boston: I. Thomas and E. T. Andrews, 1798.

———. *The Coquette*, ed. by Cathy N. Davidson. New York: Oxford University Press, 1986.

Foucault, Michel. "What Is an Author?" In *Language, Counter-memory, Practice: Selected Essays and Interviews*, ed. by Donald F. Bouchard, 113–38. New York: Cornell University Press, 1977.

Fuller, Margaret. *Women in the Nineteenth Century*. New York: Norton, 1971.

Funk, Rus. *Stopping Rape: A Challenge For Men*. Philadelphia: New Society Publishers, 1993.

Gates, Moira. *Feminism and Philosophy: Perspectives on Difference and Equality*. Bloomington: Indiana University Press, 1991.

Hansen, Klaus. "The Sentimental Novel and Its Feminist Critique." *Early American Literature* 26 (1991): 39–52.

Hartsock, Nancy. "Foucault on Power: A Theory for Women?" In *Feminism/Postmodernism*, ed. Linda J. Nicholson, 157–75. New York: Routledge, 1990.

Hindus, Michael, and Daniel Scott. "Premarital Pregnancy in America 1640–1971: An Overview and Interpretation." *Journal of Interdisciplinary History* 5 (1975): 537–70.

Hunter, Dianne, ed. *Seduction and Theory: Readings of Gender, Representation, and Rhetoric*. Chicago: University of Illinois Press, 1989.

Hymowitz, Carol, and Michaele Weissman. *A History of Women in America*. New York: Bantam Books, 1978.

Johnson, Diane. Review of *Against Our Will: Men, Women and Rape*. In *New York Review of Books* (11 December 1975): 36–37.

Jung, Carl. "On the Relation of Analytical Psychology to Poetry." In *The Spirit in Man, Art, and Literature*, ed. by Gerhard Adler, Michael Fordham, William McGuire, Herbert Read, 65–83. Princeton, NJ: Princeton University Press, 1978.

Katrak, Ketu. "Decolonizing Culture: Toward a Theory for Post-Colonial Women's Texts." In *The Post-Colonial Studies Reader*, ed. by Bill Ashcroft, Gareth Griffiths, and Helen Tiffin, 255–58. New York: Routledge, 1995.

Kerber, Linda K. *Women of the Republic: Intellect and Ideology in Revolutionary America*. Chapel Hill: University of North Carolina Press, 1980.

———. "Daughters of Columbia: Educating Women for the Republic, 1787–1805." In *Our American Sisters*, 4th ed., by Jean Friedman and Mary Jane Capozzoli, 96–114. Lexington, Mass.: D. C. Heath Company, 1987.

Koehler, Lyle. *A Search for Power*. Chicago: University of Illinois Press, 1980.

Lewis, Jan. "The Republican Wife: Virtue and Seduction in the Early Republic." *William and Mary Quarterly* 44 (1987): 689–719.

Lindemann, Barbara. "'To Ravish and Carnally Know': Rape in Eighteenth Century Massachusetts." *Signs* 10 (1984): 63–82.

Martin, Wendy. "Profile: Susanna Rowson, Early American Novelist." *Women's Studies* 2 (1974): 1–8.

McAlexander, Patricia Jewell. "The Creation of the American Eve: The Cultural Dialogue on the Nature and Role of Women in Late Eighteenth-Century America." *Early American Literature* 9 (1975): 252–75.

McDowell, Tremaine. "Sensibility in the Eighteenth Century American Novel." *Studies in Philology* 24 (1927): 383–404.

Memmi, Albert. *The Coloniser and The Colonised*. New York: Orion Press, 1965.

Miecznikowski, Cynthia J. "The Parodic Mode and the Patriarchal Imperative: Reading the Female Reader(s) in Tabitha Tenney's *Female Quixotism*." *Early American Literature* 25, no. 1 (1990): 34–45.

Miller, Jane. *Seductions: Studies in Reading and Culture*. Cambridge, Mass.: Harvard University Press, 1991.

Miller, Jean Baker. *Toward A New Psychology of Women*. Boston: Beacon Press, 1976.

Morgan, Robin. "Theory and Practice: Pornography and Rape." In *Going too Far: The Personal Chronicle of a Feminist*, 163–69. New York: Random House, 1977.

Murray, Judith Sargent. "The Gleaner Unmasked." In *The Gleaner*, ed. by Nina Baym, 804–8. Schenectady, NY: Union College Press, 1992.

———. "Industry, With The Independence Which It Confers, Celebrated and Illustrated by Facts." In *The Gleaner*, ed. by Nina Baym, 133–39. Schenectady, NY: Union College Press, 1992.

———. "Observations on Female Abilities." In *The Gleaner*, ed. by Nina Baym, 702–31. Schenectady, NY: Union College Press, 1992.

———. "On the Equality of the Sexes." *The Massachusetts Magazine* (March 1970): 132–35; and (April 1970): 223–26.

———. "Sentiments on Education." In *The Gleaner*, ed. by Nina Baym, 286–92. Schenectady, NY: Union College Press, 1992.

———. "The Story of Margaretta." In *The Gleaner*, ed. by Nina Baym. Schenectady, NY: Union College Press, 1992.

Nason, Elias. *A Memoir of Mrs. Susanna Rowson*. Albany, NY: Joel Munsell, 1870.

Norton, Mary Beth. *Liberty's Daughters: The Revolutionary Experience of American Women*. New York: Harper Collins, 1980.

Parker, Patricia. *Susanna Rowson*. Boston: Twayne, 1986.

Petter, Henri. *The Early American Novel*. Columbus, Ohio: Ohio State University Press, 1971.

Pettengill, Claire. "Sisterhood in a Separate Sphere: Female Friendship in Hannah Webster Foster's *The Coquette* and *The Boarding School*." In *Early American Literature* 27, no. 3 (1992).

Radway, Janice. *Women, Patriarchy, and Popular Literature*. Chapel Hill: University of North Carolina Press, 1984.

Reed, Toni. *Demon-Lovers and Their Victims in British Fiction*. Lexington: University of Kentucky, 1988.

Richardson, Samuel. *Clarissa* ed. by George Sherburn. Boston: Houghton Mifflin, 1962.

Robertson, Martra. *Starving in the Silences: An Exploration of Anorexia Nervosa*. New York: New York University Press, 1992.

Rossi, Alice, ed. *The Feminist Papers: From Adams to de Beauvoir*. Boston: Northeastern University Press, 1973.

Rothenberg, Paula, ed. *Race, Class, and Gender in the United States*. New York: St. Martin's Press, 1992.

Rousseau, Jean-Jacques. *Emile*. London: Dent and Sons, 1972.

Rowson, Susanna. *An Abridgment of Universal Geography, Together With Sketches of History. Designed for the Use of Schools and Academies in the United States*. Boston: John West, 1805.

———. *Charlotte Temple*, ed. by Cathy N. Davidson. New York: Oxford University Press, 1986.

———. *Charlotte Temple and Lucy Temple*, ed. by Ann Douglas. New York: Penguin Books, 1991.

———. *Exercises in History, Chronology, and Biography, in Question and Answer*. Boston: John West, 1822.

———. *The Inquisitor; or, Invisible Rambler,* vols. 1, 2, and 3. Philadelphia: William Gibbons, 1793.

———. *A Present for Young Ladies; Containing Poems, Dialogues, Addresses*. Boston: John West, 1811.

———. *Slaves in Algiers; or, a Struggle for Freedom*. Philadelphia: Wrigley and Berriman, 1794.

Rubin, Gayle. "The Traffic in Women: Notes on the Political Economy of Sex." In *Towards an Anthropology of Women*, ed. by Rayna Reiter, 157–210. New York: Monthly Review Press, 1975.

Rush, Benjamin. "Thoughts Upon Female Education." In *Essays On Education in the Early Republic*, ed. by Frederick Rudolph, 27–40. Cambridge, Mass.: Harvard University Press, 1965.

Salmon, Marylynn. "'Life, Liberty, and Dower': The Legal Status of Women After the American Revolution." In *Women, War, and Revolution*, ed. by Carol Berkin and Clara Lovett, 85–103. New York: Holmes and Meier, 1979.

Scheuermann, Mona. "The American Novel of Seduction: An Explanation of the Omission of the Sex Act in *The Scarlett Letter*." *The Nathaniel Hawthorne Journal* 8 (1978): 105–18.

"Seduction." *Webster's Ninth New Collegiate Dictionary.* Springfield, Mass.: Merriam-Webster Inc., 1994.

Shuffelton, Frank. "Mrs. Foster's *The Coquette* and the Decline of Brotherly Watch." *Studies in Eighteenth Century Culture* 16 (1986): 211–24.

Smith-Rosenberg, Carroll. "Domesticating Virtue: Coquettes and Revolutionaries in Young America." *Literature and the Body: Essays on Populations and Persons*, ed. by Elaine Scarry, 160–84. Baltimore, Md.: Johns Hopkins University Press, 1988.

Spivak, G. C. *In Other Worlds: Essays in Cultural Politics*. New York: Methuen, 1987.

Stanton, Elizabeth Cady. "Declaration of Sentiments." In *The Feminist Papers*, ed. by Alice S. Ross, 415–20. Boston: Northeastern University Press, 1971.

Stoltenberg, John. *Refusing To Be A Man: Essays on Sex and Justice*. New York: Meridian Books, 1990.

Tenney, Tabitha Gilman. *Female Quixotism*, ed. by Andrea Collins and Jean Nienkamp. New York: Oxford University Press, 1992.

Tomkins, Jane. *Sensational Designs: The Cultural Work of American Fiction, 1790–1860*. New York: Oxford University Press, 1985.

Waldstreicher, David. "Fallen Under My Observation: Vision and Virtue in *The Coquette*." *Early American Literature* 27, no. 3 (1992): 204–18.

Weil, Dorothy. *In Defense of Women: Susanna Rowson*. University Park: Pennsylvania State University Press, 1976.

Welter, Barbara. "The Cult of True Womanhood: 1820–1860." *American Quarterly* 18 (1966): 151–74.

Wenska, Walter P. "The *Coquette* and the American Dream of Freedom." *Early American Literature* 12, no. 3 (1977–78): 243–55.

Woody, Thomas. *A History of Women's Education in the United States*, vols. 1 and 2. New York: Octagon Books, 1966.

Index

culture. *See* novel; popular culture; rape culture; women

Dall, Caroline, 7n
"Daughters of Columbia" (Kerber), 30
Davidson, Cathy, 3n, 4n, 8, 23; on education reform, 2, 18; on fallen woman, 67; on Tenney, 45; on Whitman, 7n, 15
Davis, Angela, 21, 29
death formula, 1, 5, 14, 15, 26, 35
Declaration of Independence, The: excluded women, 57, 59, 72, 107, 108; rhetoric of, 69, 72, 73. *See also* Adams, John; patriarchy
Declaration of Sentiments (Stanton), 109
decolonization, 55–56, 78, 108. *See also* colonized Other
"Decolonizing Culture" (Katrak), 71
democracy: likened to Lovelace, 2, 22, 107; likened to a rake, 2, 3; and seduction, 14; Rousseau on, 79. *See also Lovelace*
depression, 97–99
"Difference of Postmodern Feminism, The" (Ebert), 44
"Domesticating Virtue" (Smith-Rosenberg), 67
double standard, 89–90
Douglas, Ann, 13–14
During, Simon, 70

Early American Novel, The (Petter), 5
Ebert, Teresa, 44
education: Boston, 29; consciousness raising via, 43, 44, 55, 109–10; curriculum reform, 25–26, 30, 31, 32, 35, 38; female, 25–31, 50; gender and, 29, 48; history as, 38–39; independence and, 81; innovations, 52; issues, 4, 6, 81; laws, 28–29; minority, 28–29; "mistaken," 28; mother's roles in, 50–51, 52; novels as part of, 38; Philadelphia, 31n; reform, 78,

109–10; school types and, 28, 30; seduction and 12, 17–19, 26, 27–28, 83, 75, 76, 106; textbooks, 26, 32; women in the workplace and, 59; women's right to, 54. *See also* novels by specific title; African American; civil rights; Foster; Murray; Rowson; Rush; self-awareness; Tenney
Eliot, John, 29
Elizabeth Whitman Mystery, The (Bolton), 7n
Emile (Rousseau) 79–80
Empire Writes Back, The, 19
Enlightenment, the, 14; Biblical roots in, 84; philosophy of, 40, 42, 51, 78, 79; rationalism, 70, 79, 89; waning, 69
Erdrich, Louise, 95
escapism, 8–9
Estes, Clarissa, 6, 61, 106
Evans, Martha Noel, 18
Exercises in History (Rowson), 49, 53

fallen woman, the: America as a, 3, 104; as a bad influence, 15–16; change and, 63–64; death outcome for, 6, 15, 26; defined, 66; depression, 97–99; fall of Eve, Eden, and, 13–15, 88; metaphors to emphasize, 76; 19th century writing and, 109; outcome of, 63; Puritanism and, 101; redemption for a, 102; as a religious figure, 103; seduction theme and, 107; speech and identity for, 104; stereotypes and, 73, 95, 96–97, 100–1, 104, 105; suicide for the, 103–4; Tenney's, 66; theme, 3, 5, 6, 66, 69; transcending prescribed roles by, 70–71. *See also Charlotte Temple; Coquette; Female Quixotism; Lucy Temple*
Fasting Girls (Brumberg), 102, 103–4
fate in the seduction novel, 14, 35–36, 57, 69, 88. *See also Coquette*; predestination